DISCARD

THE VANISHING AMERICAN CORPORATION

THE VANISHING AMERICAN CORPORATION

NAVIGATING THE HAZARDS OF A NEW ECONOMY

Gerald F. Davis

Berrett–Koehler Publishers, Inc.
a BK Currents book

Berrett-Koehler Publishers, Inc.
1333 Broadway, Suite 1000
Oakland, CA 94612-1921
Tel: (510) 817-2277   Fax: (510) 817-2278   www.bkconnection.com

Ordering Information

Quantity sales. Special discounts are available on quantity purchases by corporations, associations, and others. For details, contact the "Special Sales Department" at the Berrett-Koehler address above.

Individual sales. Berrett-Koehler publications are available through most bookstores. They can also be ordered directly from Berrett-Koehler: Tel: (800) 929-2929; Fax: (802) 864-7626; www.bkconnection.com

Orders for college textbook/course adoption use. Please contact Berrett-Koehler: Tel: (800) 929-2929; Fax: (802) 864-7626.

Orders by U.S. trade bookstores and wholesalers. Please contact Ingram Publisher Services, Tel: (800) 509-4887; Fax: (800) 838-1149; E-mail: customer.service @ingrampublisherservices.com; or visit www.ingrampublisherservices.com/Ordering for details about electronic ordering.

Berrett-Koehler and the BK logo are registered trademarks of Berrett-Koehler Publishers, Inc.

Printed in the United States of America

Berrett-Koehler books are printed on long-lasting acid-free paper. When it is available, we choose paper that has been manufactured by environmentally responsible processes. These may include using trees grown in sustainable forests, incorporating recycled paper, minimizing chlorine in bleaching, or recycling the energy produced at the paper mill.

Library of Congress Cataloging-in-Publication Data

Names: Davis, Gerald F. (Gerald Fredrick), 1961– author.
Title: The vanishing American corporation : navigating the hazards of a new economy / Gerald F. Davis, The University of Michigan.
Description: First edition. | Oakland : Berrett-Koehler Publishers, [2016] | Includes bibliographical references and index.
Identifiers: LCCN 2015050640 | ISBN 9781626562790 (hardcover)
Subjects: LCSH: Corporations--United States--History. | Industries--United States--History. | United States--Economic conditions.
Classification: LCC HD2785 .D26 2016 | DDC 338.7/40973--dc23
LC record available at http://lccn.loc.gov/2015050640

First Edition
21 20 19 18 17 16   10 9 8 7 6 5 4 3 2 1

Book production and design: Seventeenth Street Studios
Copyeditor: Laurie Dunne
Indexer: Richard Evans
Cover designer: Seventeenth Street Studios
Illustration: Valerie Winemiller, Seventeenth Street Studios
Author Photo: Ross School of Business

TO BEN AND GRACE, *as they join the new Powerball economy*

CONTENTS

PREFACE

HY WOULD ANYONE want to write a gloomy book about the economy? And who would want to read it?

As a business professor who sees a lot of examples, I can attest that the world does not need another dull and jargon-filled book about business. But my motivation for writing this book was more personal. I wanted to give some advice to kids heading off into the world, including my own. Yet I was stumped.

When I headed to college, the options were clear. If you studied something practical, like engineering or business, you could get a corporate job when you finished school. If you studied something frivolous like philosophy, as I did, you could go to law school. And if you ran out of money and dropped out, there was always the chance of getting a union job on the assembly line.

That was in the early 1980s. In the years since then, we have all learned about the death of the corporate career. The company would not take care of you; you had to navigate from job to job and company to company, sometimes shifting laterally, but over the long run moving ahead. Today, even the "job" is endangered. Kids graduating from college might find themselves juggling an unpaid internship with a part-time job as a dog sitter and an intermittent gig driving for Uber.

If you ever played the children's game Chutes and Ladders, you have a pretty good idea of the economic landscape facing millennials today. A handful land at the right place at the right time and manage to move up—maybe even selling their app to Facebook and retiring before age 30. But the vast majority face a precarious labor market where one wrong step might send them down the chute to part-time purgatory, struggling to put together enough shifts to make their student loan payments. The factories haven't been hiring for years, and law school only leads to a higher class of unemployment. Even the computer literate working for brand-name corporations find that their jobs can be done more cheaply offshore (sometimes after they train their own replacements).

At the same time, the American corporation has been undergoing dramatic and puzzling changes. The shift from *careers* to *jobs* to *tasks* corresponds to a change in the shape of the corporate economy. Corporate careers only make sense when you have corporations that last a long time. But the "gales of creative destruction" beloved by business writers seem to be a lot heavier on the destruction than on the creation. The most venerable names in the corporate economy were going bankrupt (General Motors, Chrysler, Eastman Kodak), morphing into new industries (Westinghouse, Woolworth), splitting into component parts (Alcoa, Hewlett-Packard, Time Warner), or disappearing entirely (Bethlehem Steel, Lehman Brothers, Borders, Circuit City, and many others). The number of American companies listed on the stock market dropped by more than half between 1997 and 2012. Moreover, new entrants like Zynga and Zillow and Zulily start small and never grow big. By relying on contractors rather than hiring permanent employees in bulk, the newest corporations seem destined to remain tiny.

The new businesses in the "sharing economy" have dispensed with employment almost entirely. At the end of 2014 Uber had over 160,000 "driver-partners" in the United States but only about 2,000 actual employees. Similar figures hold for Airbnb and other "sharing" firms. They are not manufacturers or service providers but *platforms*, out to disrupt traditional industries such as taxis, hotels, and even medicine. In school I was often threatened with suspension for being disruptive. Now being disruptive is an essential virtue for any new business plan.

These things are connected.

New technologies enable new ways of doing business and new forms of organization. New ways of doing business change the economic landscape and the prospects that individuals and families face. In the 20th century, the American economy was dominated by major corporations. In the 21st, that will no longer be true. The old maps no longer work for our emerging economy, and the old remedies no longer fix current problems. The steam engine allowed factories to operate anywhere that could obtain coal, and drove the first industrial revolution. It gave us the steamship, the locomotive, and more globalized markets, as well as the "dark Satanic mills," as William Blake described them, and the urban bedlam of Dickens. The mass production methods that shrank the cost of the Model T spread to all realms of industrial society over the 20th century, from how children were educated to how war was conducted. They gave us the modern corporation, the modern labor movement, and the American way of life. The Web and the smartphone allow pervasive markets and spontaneous collaborations at minimal cost. They make institutions like the modern corporation increasingly unsustainable. What comes next is up to us.

When the corporate economy arose in the early 20th century, astute observers like Theodore Roosevelt recognized that it created both opportunities for prosperity and hazards for democracy. Roosevelt and other Progressives recognized the need for well-informed public policy to harness the new corporations for public benefit.

Today we face a set of challenges similar to those at the turn of the last century: rising inequality, lower mobility, a ragged social safety net, and politics dominated by the wealthy. But this time the cause is not the *growth* of the corporate sector, but its *collapse*. If we want to build an economy that works for all and that provides opportunities to the young, we need to start with an accurate diagnosis of our current situation. *The Vanishing American Corporation* is my venture at such a diagnosis.

I want to thank several readers who gave generous comments on this manuscript as it evolved. They include J. Adam Cobb, David Drews, Wallace Katz, Maggie Levenstein, Dana Muir, and Niels Selling; three excellent Berrett-Koehler reviewers: Jeffrey Kulick, Robert Ellman, and Michael S. Brady; and particularly Steve Piersanti, who shepherded this book with care and expertise from its very earliest stage, in spite of my serial deadline prevarications. Working with Berrett-Koehler has been a delight from start to finish. As always, I also thank my delightful spouse Christina Brown for her endless cheer and encouragement. I hope the final product justified her faith.

TECTONIC SHIFTS AND THE NEW ECONOMIC LANDSCAPE

I N AN ERA of *Citizens United* and eight-figure paychecks for CEOs, it is easy to imagine that corporations have never been more powerful. Yet public corporations—companies that sell shares to the public, rather than being privately owned—are in retreat in the United States. The number of American companies listed on the stock market has dropped by more than half in the past 15 years, as departures outnumber initial public offerings (IPOs) almost every year. Some of this is due to economic crises and industry consolidation, but most of it is caused by the increasing obsolescence of the corporate form.

For many traditionally "corporate" activities, organizing as a corporation and listing shares on a stock market is no longer the most cost-effective way to do business. Tiny Vizio can sell televisions much more cheaply than giant Sony. The maker of Flip, with 100 employees, sold more portable video cameras than century-old Eastman Kodak, before both became obsolete. Uber has more "driver-partners" in the US than General Motors has employees. Outside of a few industries with very large capital requirements, the sustainability of the traditional corporate form is increasingly in question.

The claim that corporations are in decline is surprising, to say the least. Who can doubt the majestic power of Walmart or Goldman Sachs or Google or McDonalds? Corporations have been dominant economic institutions for over a century, providing products and services as well as jobs for workers and profits for investors. Yet in industry after industry, noncorporate forms are thriving, and corporations are struggling, as the economies of scale that sustained corporations erode. In 1950 it might have made economic sense to assemble cars in giant vertically integrated factories in Detroit and ship them from there to the rest of the world. Today, the parts of a business are like interlocking plastic bricks that can be snapped together temporarily and snapped apart when they are no longer needed. Information and communication technologies (ICTs) make starting an enterprise trivially easy, from creating a legal structure to hiring temporary employees to contracting out for production and distribution. Coordinating activities used to be the corporation's strong suit. Now the corporation is increasingly out-maneuvered by alternative forms of enterprise that are more flexible and less costly. The barriers to entry are falling across a wide swathe of industries.

In his famous 1937 article "The Nature of the Firm," Nobel Prize-winning economist Ronald Coase explained, "The main reason why it is profitable to establish a firm would seem to be that there is a cost of using the price system. The most obvious cost of 'organising' production through the price mechanism is that of discovering what the relevant prices are." But what if discovering the relevant prices becomes trivial? What if the inputs of a firm, including labor, can be priced and ordered as they are needed? What if, in place of long-term employees, firms were able to contract for workers if and when they were needed for specific tasks—the way that customers can use the Uber app to order a ride? This is the world that is emerging now. And while the result may be a delight for consumers, who benefit from low prices and new conveniences, it will become a disaster for labor.

After World War II, Americans relied on corporate employers for their incomes, retirement security, and health insurance for their families. Corporations not only created products and services, but pathways to move up in the world. Whatever their faults, corporations were a source of economic opportunity and stability for workers. Today, the compact between corporations and employees is increasingly under siege by low-cost alternatives that make the traditional corporation unsustainable.

This does not mean that business will disappear, but that its organizational shape will change. Indeed, companies continue to list shares on the market and to attract the attention of investors, albeit at a far lower rate than in prior decades. But they are very different from those that came before. Companies going public around the turn of the 20th century included General Electric, Westinghouse, US Steel, and Eastman Kodak, which grew to be pillars of the 20th-century economy. IPO companies in more recent years occasionally create shareholder value, but they rarely create jobs in large numbers. At this writing, the combined global workforces of Facebook, Yelp, Zynga, LinkedIn, Zillow, Tableau, Zulily, and Box are smaller than the number of people who lost their jobs when Circuit City was liquidated in 2009. Throw in Google and it's still less than the number who worked at Blockbuster in 2005. There is little reason to expect these new technology firms to grow into century-spanning institutions like Kodak or Westinghouse.

Corporations will survive in some sectors, just as there are still royal families in Denmark, Spain, and the United Kingdom. But they will be vestigial rather than central pillars of the economy, and they will not provide stable employment on a large scale. Exxon, one of the world's most long-lasting and financially successful corporations, had 150,000 employees in 1962 (when it was still Standard Oil of New Jersey). Fifty years later, after merging with its giant rival Mobil, it had half as many.

The decline of the corporation is most evident in the US, but the underlying factors behind it are visible around the world. Information technologies are drastically lowering the costs of using the price system. Capital equipment gets radically cheaper and more powerful every year; the Web and mobile phones greatly lower the costs of coordination and collaboration. Corporations are thus no longer the inevitable way to organize an advanced economy. The US became the most corporatized economy early in the 20th century, creating a path that many other economies ultimately followed. Today, the US is the furthest advanced in de-corporatizing. This is, perhaps, the canary in the coal mine. American multinationals have a habit of spreading best (or non-best) practices to their operations around the world, and it is possible that the decline of corporations will spread as well.

The consequences of corporate decline in the US are stark: increased inequality, decreased mobility, and a frayed social safety net. It is hard to fathom where power resides in our economy today, and harder still to know how to navigate it. The generation of those under 30 faces crushing college debt and a rocky economic landscape governed by inscrutable rules. The generation about to retire faces insecurity about financing for their health care and pensions.

The Vanishing American Corporation provides a systematic account of the disappearance of the corporation in the US and its implications. Most of us still understand our economy using an outdated map that sees corporations as the dominant feature of the economic landscape. My hope is to provide a map that renders our current situation more legible, for citizens, businesspeople, and policymakers. Unless we understand the tectonic shifts underway, we will not be able to address them and build an economy that works for all.

THE CORPORATE CENTURY IN AMERICA

THE CORPORATE CENTURY IN AMERICA

THE 20TH CENTURY was the corporate century in America. The American economy became "corporatized" around the turn of the century, and for the next several decades corporations were the most important institutions in the economy, providing goods and services, jobs, and profits for investors. Yet corporations look very different around the world compared to the United States, reflecting the politics and history of their home countries. Much like "breakfast," in which the same word refers to very different things in different cultures, "corporation" means something quite different in the US, Germany, Korea, or China. For much of the past century, public corporations, with shares traded on stock markets, have been far more important to the American economy than to other economies, such as Germany, where smaller family-owned businesses play an important role. There are many ways to do business that do not involve corporations—"corporation" is not synonymous with "business."

The American public corporation grew up around mass production and mass distribution, enabled by a continent-sized consumer market. Economies of scale meant that bigger was more efficient. It also meant that corporations required capital on a scale too large to be funded by private partnerships or banks: They needed shareholders. Massive size was a distinguishing feature of the American corporation for most of the 20th century, and big firms were almost always listed on the stock market.

Large national corporations and their bankers created a worrisome aggregation of power in the early 20th century. The Progressive movement advocated the expansion of a federal government powerful enough to act as a counterweight to the new corporations, including regulatory agencies such as the Food and Drug Administration and new cabinet-level departments like the Department of Labor. The growth of a large national government went hand in hand with the growth of the corporation.

After the labor laws of the 1930s, the mobilization for World War II, and postwar labor agreements across major industries, the American corporation emerged with a widely shared social compact that included stable employment, career ladders, and benefits, such as health insurance and retirement security for employees and their families. This corresponded with an era of unprecedented prosperity, low inequality, and high mobility, largely underwritten by the corporate economy. For three decades after the end of the war, American corporations continued to grow bigger and more encompassing.

CHAPTER 1

CORPORATIONS IN AMERICA AND AROUND THE WORLD

WE LIVE OUR lives surrounded by corporations and their products. At home, at work, in public places, we see their brands (Coca-Cola), eat their food (McDonalds), use their products (Apple), track their share prices, and use their names as verbs (Google, Xerox). It seems that corporations rule the world.

This book makes a surprising claim: Corporations are in decline, and are reaching the end of their reign in the United States. This is surprising for many reasons. Public corporations (those that sell shares on the stock market) have been the most important institutions in the American economy for more than a century.[1] Corporations are the biggest employers and produce the biggest part of our economic output. Most American households own shares in American corporations, and many depend on these investments to fund their retirement and their children's college expenses.[2] Corporations are also deeply involved in the American political system, using their economic power to promote policies that favor their interests. Love them or hate them, public corporations seem indispensable.

We tend to think of corporations as a permanent part of the landscape, like a mountain range that has always been there. But corporations are more like the palace at Versailles where King Louis held court. The monarchy in France seemed eternal, endowed by God with the authority to rule. Yet over the course of a few months during the French Revolution, the monarchy and its associated institutions fell. Things that had been taken for granted for generations—even the names of the months and the units of measure—were up for grabs.

I argue in this book that we are in a situation like that now. Corporations in many domains have outlived their usefulness, and their decline will bring about major shifts in American life, from how we earn a living to how we get health care to whether we can afford to retire.

This chapter provides the background for the rest of the book by explaining what a corporation is, why it looks different in different countries, and why they are changing. Although many people think of "corporate" as a synonym for "business," the corporation is a very specific way of doing business, and the public corporation is a special type of corporation. We want to be clear on our terms before we dive in too far.

What is a corporation?

THE WORD "CORPORATION" calls to mind images of hierarchy, money, and power. If asked to draw a corporation, many people would sketch an organization chart shaped like a steeply pitched pyramid. At the apex would be a middle-aged white guy with a thick head of hair, clad in an expensive suit, looking something like Alec Baldwin without the smirk.

For Americans, General Motors in its heyday might serve as an appropriate stand-in for the corporation. At its peak GM had nearly a million employees, from the vast unionized workforce operating its countless factories to an enormous white-collar office staff occupying its headquarters tower in Detroit. GM was the world's largest manufacturer, with outposts around the world making cars around the clock. When the first Fortune 500 list was published in 1955, GM was at the top. In *Modern Times*, Charlie Chaplin provided an indelible image of the industrial worker at a company like GM, trapped in the gears of the corporation both physically and metaphorically.

Most of us think of the corporation as a specific kind of organization. When presidential candidate Mitt Romney told a heckler that "corporations are people, my friend," he expressed the sense that corporations are simply a group of people—sometimes very large—trying to do business together.[3]

If you ask a lawyer, however, you will learn that a corporation is simply a legal device with a few features that are useful for contracts and financing. Corporations generally have limited liability, legal "personality," and unlimited lifespan. *Limited liability* means that when people do business with a corporation, such as lending it money, they understand that it is the corporation as an entity that owes them money, not the corporation's owners or managers. If the company goes bust, lenders can't show up at the shareholders' houses and start carting away their furniture. However, limited liability does *not* mean that corporations or their owners and employees are not legally liable for their actions. An executive who commits a crime in the name of the corporation is still a criminal.

Legal personality means that the corporation can "sign" contracts and own things, just like a person. The corporation is not just a group of people, but has its own peculiar existence separate from them. Legal personality does *not* mean that corporations have rights identical to actual human beings.

Unlimited lifespan means that corporations can be maintained by different people and can last indefinitely. All of a corporation's employees and shareholders can change, but it is still the same corporation.

Corporations are useful for many purposes, not just business. Nonprofit organizations and municipalities are often legally organized as corporations. One of the most famous legal cases in history, *Trustees of Dartmouth College v. Woodward*, decided by the US Supreme Court in 1819, laid out the legal status of the corporation—in this case, Dartmouth College and the sanctity of its contracts.[4] A change in personnel does not automatically mean a change in the corporation's status or contractual obligations.

Corporations differ from other kinds of organizations and legal entities in important ways. The things that distinguish corporations determine very practical matters, such as who or what pays the taxes and who/what is financially liable or is being lent to.

In spite of their special legal status, corporations are easy to create and destroy. You can create a corporation right now by visiting the Liberian Corporate Registry at the website http://liberiancorporations. com/corporate-entities/corporation/forms/. You would not be alone in "virtual Liberia": Miami-based Royal Caribbean Cruises is incorporated in Liberia, as are a number of other companies that reside physically in America, which find substantial tax advantages in maintaining Liberian citizenship.[5]

Some big businesses are not "corporations" at all. After it was sold by Daimler, automaker Chrysler—with $50 billion in revenues and 72,000 employees—was an LLC, not an Inc. An LLC is a "limited liability company," which is a sort of legal mash-up between a corporation and a partnership. The LLC has grown to be perhaps the most widely used legal form of business organization in the US (and can be owned by parent corporations, such as Amazon Services, LLC, owned by Amazon.com, Inc.). The late legal scholar Larry Ribstein labeled the LLC and other formats "uncorporations" to distinguish them from traditional corporations and partnerships. LLCs are typically cheaper to establish than a corporation (in some states as low as $50), highly flexible, and have certain tax advantages, as well as offering limited liability to their owners.

The distinction between a "corporation" and an "LLC" or other legal form may seem trivial, but there are good reasons why LLCs have become so popular and corporations are in decline. One is regulation: When Congress wants business to behave, it often does so by passing securities laws that are only relevant for corporations listed on the stock market. The Foreign Corrupt Practices Act (aimed at preventing companies from paying bribes) and the Dodd-Frank Act (which requires companies to disclose if their products contain "conflict minerals" that could fund atrocities in the Democratic Republic of Congo) are examples that apply to listed corporations but not (in general) to LLCs. Although we will not focus on LLCs in this book, their popularity makes it clear that there are a lot of legal formats for business that are not corporations.[6]

The corporations that we will be concerned with in this book are "public corporations," the biggest and most visible form of organization. Most of the companies that people call to mind when they think of business are public corporations: GM, Apple, Walmart, Exxon, Coca-Cola. *Public* is a slightly confusing term here, because it does not mean "owned by the broad public" (like a national park) but "having ownership shares traded on stock markets." It is "public" in the sense that the public can buy and sell shares (in contrast to, say, a partnership or family-owned company). When companies "go public" or make an "initial public offering" (IPO), they are making shares available for purchase on a stock market. At this point, if they are American companies, they are almost inevitably organized as corporations under the laws of one of the 50 states (usually Delaware, for reasons to be explained later).

For almost the entire 20th century, public corporations such as AT&T and General Motors controlled the bulk of economic activity in America. The decline of these corporations is the topic of this book.

"Corporation" and "business" are not the same thing

IN EVERYDAY USAGE, "corporate" often refers to anything having to do with business, finance, or money. Almost any business larger than a mom-and-pop store will be regarded as corporate, even if (as in the case of most McDonald's outlets in the US) it is a partnership, family-owned business, or other form.[7] Perhaps due to the widespread corporatization of the economy for much of the 20th century, commerce is seen as corporate unless proved otherwise.

Corporate is often used as an epithet. When we say someone has "gone corporate," we mean that they have started wearing a suit, greeting people with a handshake, and nattering on about value added and leveraging and core competences. Music is corporate when it is soulless, slick, and overproduced. "Corporate" is the antonym of "indie" or "alt."

But it is worth being precise when talking about corporations. When commentators worry about "corporate money" dominating politics, they often mean that wealthy people (and the shadowy organizations that they fund) have too much influence. The Koch Brothers often serve as poster children for corporate influence, even though Koch Industries—the source of their wealth—is a privately owned business, not a public corporation.[8]

Does it really matter if a hedge-fund billionaire gains his or her wealth through an LLC chartered in the Cayman Islands rather than through a Delaware corporation traded on the New York Stock Exchange? The answer is yes. Corporations, particularly those listed on stock markets, really are different in essential ways from other ways of doing business, from how they are funded and taxed to whom they owe obligations and legal responsibilities. This is why Michael Dell and his colleagues were willing to go to great expense to take Dell Computer private (that is, to buy out all its shares and de-list it from the stock market).[9] Public corporations face greater scrutiny and more extensive regulation than other kinds of business. Companies that need to undergo substantial restructurings, or want to avoid scrutiny, have reasons to avoid being public. Put another way, it is often easier for the government to shape the actions of public corporations than private companies. This matters for public policy and our ability as a nation to guide corporations to behave themselves.

Corporations look different around the world

HOW IS THE corporation like breakfast? The question sounds cryptic, but consider the range of foods that count as breakfast around the world. In Sweden, it might be smoked fish and dark bread. In Korea, soup and rice. In France, a croissant with preserves. In Israel, fresh salads and fish. In Switzerland, muesli and yogurt. In Canada, pancakes and maple syrup. And England's hapless citizens are forced to eat sausages, eggs, and baked beans first thing in the morning.

Other than being the first meal of the day, "breakfast" seems to mean wildly different things around the world. Calling a meal "breakfast" provides surprisingly little information about what kind of food will be served, and only slightly more information about *when* it will be served. The same is true of the corporation. Although we might expect some basic similarities among the world's corporations, we would be wrong, as even the most successful industrial economies host quite different kinds of corporations.

Start at the top: What should the board of directors look like? Boards of directors oversee the broad operations of the corporation and are ultimately responsible for its activities and performance. Given the globalization of financial markets, one might expect best practices in corporate governance to be fairly standardized for the world's largest corporations. Yet in the US, a corporate board typically contains roughly 10 members—the Chief Executive Officer, Chief Financial Officer, and eight unaffiliated outsiders. For instance, GM's board has only one insider and eleven outsiders, comprised largely of retired CEOs.[10] In Japan, a board might have twice as many members as in the US, with a large majority being company insiders. At Toyota 12 of the 15 directors are current or former executives of the company.[11] German corporations are legally required to have half of their supervisory board elected by the employees, to ensure that labor is represented in corporate decision making. This is true at Daimler, where 10 of the 20 board members are elected by employees.[12] And China's Geely Automotive board includes eight executive and six nonexecutive directors.[13]

In short, even among the world's four largest and most successful economies, there is no shared standard for how the board of directors should look, even within the same industry. The same is true all the way down: Like breakfast, corporations look very different around the world.

Countries also differ greatly in their number of stock market-listed companies, and even in whether they have corporations at all. We tend to think of the corporation as an unstoppable invasive species, spreading like bamboo, but in some sense it is more like an orchid, requiring very specific conditions to thrive. Half of the world's economies do not even have stock markets, which rules out the possibility of public corporations. Of those economies that do have stock markets, half have had them for less than 30 years.[14] The collapse of the Soviet Union left former communist countries with the problem of how to transition from government ownership to privately held ownership on a massive scale. Thus, in a brief period, stock markets erupted all over Eastern Europe thanks to "mass privatization," in which marketable shares in state-owned enterprises were handed over to the public. The People's Republic of China had no stock market from the Revolution in 1949 until 1990; the Shanghai Stock Exchange is now one of the largest in the world.

Yet corporations are neither necessary nor sufficient for economic vibrancy. Countries can have vibrant economies with few corporations, or they can have weak economies with many corporations. Thailand had 613 public corporations in 2014, according to the World Bank. Germany, whose economy was almost 10 times larger than Thailand, had only 595. The Netherlands, birthplace of the modern stock exchange, had 130. Vietnam, a more recent convert, had 305.[15] It is, in short, entirely possible to have strong, export-oriented economies with few corporations. On the other hand, a large corporate sector is no guarantee of economic vitality.

Corporations look the way they do because of their country's history and institutions. Corporations grow up at different points in a country's development. American corporations emerged during the railroad era and developed with manufacturing firms around the turn of the 20th century, when there was a lot of uncertainty about what a corporation ought to look like. Through trial and error, they came to look the way we know them today. In contrast, Korean corporations developed in the 1950s and 1960s and were able to draw on proven models from other countries. Korea adapted the corporation to its own particular needs over a number of years, guided by a broad agenda of economic development after the Korean War. In contrast, former Eastern Bloc economies adopted entirely new formats of corporate economy more or less overnight with the breakup of the Soviet Union. In some cases, this was successful; in others, it was disastrous, as the officials responsible for managing the transition from communism to capitalism found it to be an opportunity for looting on a world-historical scale. Dynastic fortunes were created overnight, but it would be hard to see this as a triumph of free markets.

Just as local architecture is shaped by the traditions and raw materials of a region, corporate structures are shaped by aspects of the economy and society. Scholars have found that five broad factors are particularly important for shaping the kinds of corporations and other businesses a country gets, and why corporations look so different around the world. These factors include how the *labor market* works; how critical *financial markets* are to funding businesses; how *product market competition* is encouraged or regulated; the organization of the *education system*; and the character of the *social safety net*, including things like health insurance, unemployment insurance, and pensions.[16]

In the US, for instance, corporate employers after World War II provided health insurance and retirement security, which has resulted in workers dependent on particular employers and created expenses for firms that they do not bear elsewhere. American corporations have elaborate human resource functions to deal with these requirements, and an army of bureaucrats to regulate them. In Denmark, on the other hand, the national government assures access to health care and retirement security regardless of employment status, making it less costly to start up new businesses, and less risky to work for them.

Efforts to transfer practices or institutions from other countries are often doomed to fail because they require a supporting "ecosystem" to work. "Why can't you be more like Germany, with its thriving export-oriented manufacturing sector?" German manufacturing firms benefit from a strong vocational education system that trains skilled workers for entry-level jobs; a tradition of labor-management collaboration; family ownership coupled with bank financing rather than market financing; a long-standing orientation toward selling on global markets rather than just domestic markets; and a well-established social welfare system that encourages employees to invest in skill development. Just as it's hard to grow coffee in Canada because of its soil and climate, it's hard to grow German-style manufacturing firms in the US because we do not have the right institutional ecosystem for German-style firms. Notably, a handful of German firms like BMW are attempting to replicate parts of their traditional ecosystem (such as vocational training) in exotic places like South Carolina.

The corporation in America

TO A GREATER degree than almost any other country, the United States has had a corporatized economy for generations. From early in the 20th century, corporations controlled most of the nation's economic assets and employed the bulk of the labor force.[17]

Individual corporations dwarfed the size of other social institutions. In 1910, US Steel's assets were far larger than the federal government's annual budget.[18] By 1930, a mere 200 corporations controlled half of the nation's corporate assets.[19] Commentators at the time stated that corporations were more similar to nation-states than to traditional family-owned businesses. When GM's CEO (and later Secretary of Defense) told Congress in 1953 that "what was good for the country was good for General Motors, and vice versa," it was not meant arrogantly or sarcastically.[20] The health of the economy and the health of the largest corporations were inextricably tied. To a great extent, particularly after World War II, the largest corporations *were* the economy.

But if the corporation is the foundation of the American economy, we need to be concerned. GM had about as many employees in 2015 as it did in 1928, which was just one-fourth of its size in the 1980s (see Figure 1.1). Its total North American workforce today is about as large as the number employed at Ford's famous River Rouge plant in the 1930s.

An optimist might suggest that those jobs have simply shifted to other, growing industries, such as computers and electronics. Yet according to the Bureau of Labor Statistics, employment in the

FIGURE 1.1 Employment at GM in thousands, 1923–2009

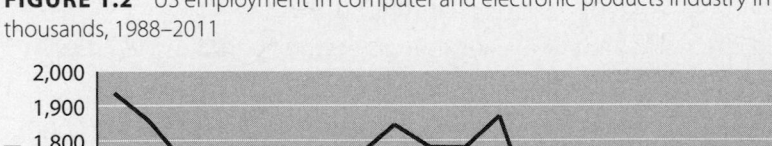

Source: Data from *Moody's Industrial Manual* (various years), Compustat, form 10-K

computer and electronics industry has actually *shrunk dramatically* since 2000, dropping 750,000 American jobs (see Figure 1.2). Telecommunications and information services? Nope: They had one million fewer jobs in 2013 than in 2000 (see Figure 1.3).[21]

In fact, the number of public corporations has collapsed in recent years. In 2012 the US had less than half as many public corporations as it did in 1997 (see Figure 1.4).[22] As we will see, this is not simply

FIGURE 1.2 US employment in computer and electronic products industry in thousands, 1988–2011

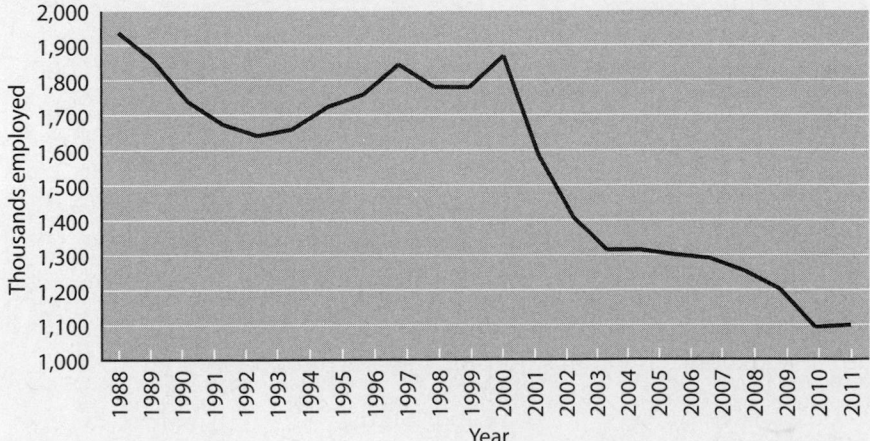

Source: Bureau of Labor Statistics

FIGURE 1.3 US employment in information sector in thousands, 1990–2012

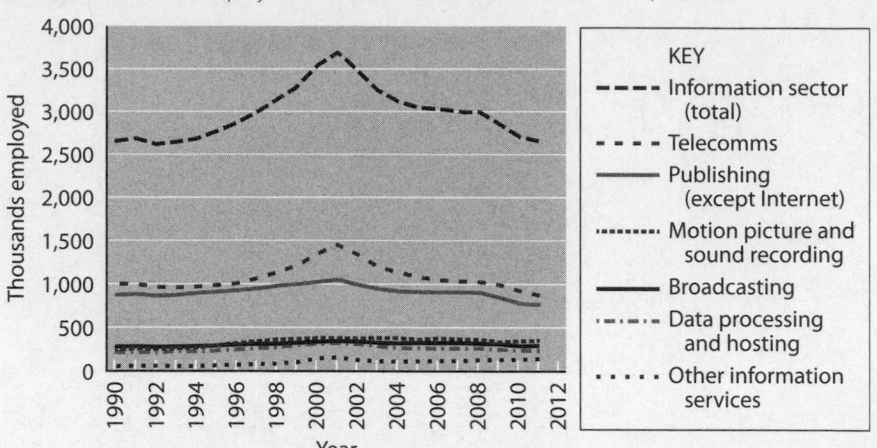

Source: Bureau of Labor Statistics

due to consolidation and mergers. Westinghouse, ITT, Eastman Kodak, Circuit City, Blockbuster, Borders, Lehman Brothers, Washington Mutual, and many other household names are gone (or mere stubs of their former selves), and they are not coming back.

This book argues that the corporation is not an eternal institution but a transient one, at least in the long sweep of history. Corporations survive if they have an economic rationale and their revenues can cover their expenses. They are not supernatural beings like vampires (their unlimited lifespan notwithstanding). If they can't cover their costs, and there are better ways of doing what corporations did, they will eventually die. If Netflix, with 2,000 employees, can provide videos more cost effectively than Blockbuster, which had over 80,000 employees in 2004, then Blockbuster will perish.[23] As we will see, the winner need not be a corporation, or even a for-profit business: If the nonprofit Wikipedia does a better job than *Encyclopedia Britannica*, then the 240-year-old institution will close (unless it finds a sugar daddy indifferent to profit). There is no crying in baseball, and there is no sentimentality in the corporate world.

The major claim of this book is that the public corporation fit well with the requirements for doing business in the 20th century,

FIGURE 1.4   Domestic companies listed on US stock markets, 1991–2014

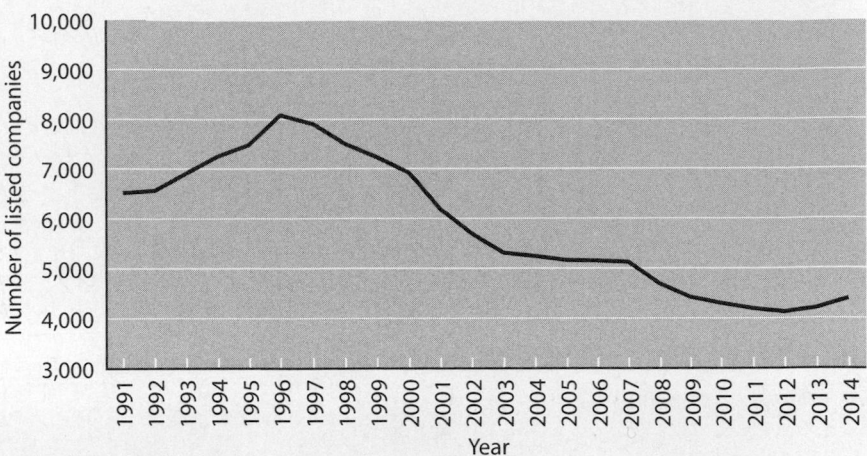

Source: World Bank, *World Development Indicators*, 2014

but it is an increasingly bad fit for 21st-century business. Corporations are tools for getting things done under particular circumstances, like monarchies, or diesel trucks. Although we might treat the corporation with reverence as a social institution, like the church or the family, it is primarily an economic institution, and one whose time—at least in many domains of economic life—may have passed.

CHAPTER 2

HOW THE CORPORATION CONQUERED AMERICA

THE CORPORATE ECONOMY we know today can seem like an eternal feature of the landscape, an economic mountain range that has always been there. Yet the modern corporation emerged in a relatively brief period around the turn of the 20th century.

Consider the birth years of some of America's industry-leading corporations: AT&T (1885), Eastman Kodak (1888), General Electric (1892), Sears Roebuck (1893), US Steel (1901), General Motors (1908), and IBM (1911). The roughly two decades surrounding the turn of the century were a remarkable period: Dozens of business empires that spanned the globe for a century were born. It was like a Cambrian explosion in which a vast diversity of new species appeared in the blink of an eye.

Prior to 1890, most corporations listed on stock markets in the United States were railroads and other infrastructure businesses.[1] The precursor to the Dow Jones Industrial Index included 10 railroads, Pacific Mail (a steamship operator), and Western Union (a telegraph).[2] The robber barons of the time—Vanderbilt, Gould, Stanford, Harriman—generally made their fortunes in railroads. Andrew Carnegie was a notable exception, as his namesake company was the largest steel producer in the US. In spite of its relatively vast size, however, Carnegie Steel was a partnership, not a public corporation. John D. Rockefeller made his fortune through the Standard Oil Company, but again, the vehicle was a trust controlled by a handful of families, not a public corporation.

After some initial tumult, a handful of major corporations emerged and maintained a dominant position for generations. Consider who was listed in the Dow Jones Index of "blue chips" at different points. The first Dow Jones Industrial Index in 1896 included 12 leaders of the emerging industrial economy: American Cotton Oil, American Sugar, American Tobacco, Chicago Gas, Distilling & Cattle Feeding, General Electric, Laclede Gas, National Lead, North American, Tennessee Coal & Iron, US Leather, and US Rubber. Nine years later, two-thirds of the Dow Index had turned over; 10 years after that, the churn had begun to settle down. By the early 1930s, the Index contained the familiar stable blue chips that would represent American capitalism for much of the 20th century (see Table 2.1).[3] Indeed, most corporations included in the Index in 1932 were still there 55 years later in 1987.

Mass production, mass distribution, and the "economics of big"

THE STANDARD ACCOUNT of the rise of the large corporation in the US is Alfred Chandler's *The Visible Hand*.[4] Chandler, a business historian, won a Pulitzer Prize for History for this book in 1978. He describes a combination of elements that came together at a particular time to make the familiar large, hierarchical corporation possible, if not inevitable.

What made the dawn of the 20th century so fruitful for the large corporation in America? Over the course of the 19th century the US expanded from the Atlantic to the Pacific, and in the second half the continent was spanned with a network of railroads and telegraphs. In combination this created a vast national market united by a common language and government as well as a means for the distribution of goods. Europe, in contrast, consisted of a large number of smaller national markets and no common tongue.

Meanwhile, technological advances in steelmaking and then in other industries created "economies of scale," meaning that bigger was cheaper. One giant mill making 10,000 tons of steel was cheaper than

TABLE 2.1 The Dow Jones Industrial Index, 1896–1987

1896	1905	1916	1932	1987
American Cotton Oil	Amalgamated Copper	American Beet Sugar	Allied Chemical	**Allied-Signal (Allied Chemical)***
American Sugar	American Car & Foundry	American Can	American Can	ALCOA
American Tobacco	American Smelting & Refining	American Car & Foundry	American Smelting	**American Can**
Chicago Gas Distilling & Cattle Feeding	American Sugar	American Locomotive	American Tobacco	American Express
General Electric	Colorado Fuel & Iron	American Smelting	Bethlehem Steel	AT&T
Laclede Gas	National Lead	America Sugar	Borden	**Bethlehem Steel**
National Lead	Peoples Gas	American Telephone & Telegraph (AT&T)	Chrysler	Boeing
North American	Tennessee Coal & Iron	Anaconda Copper	Coca-Cola	**Chevron**
Tennessee Coal & Iron	US Rubber	Baldwin Locomotive	Drug Inc.	**Coca-Cola**
US Leather	US Rubber pfd.	Central Leather	Eastman Kodak	DuPont
US Rubber	US Steel	General Electric	General Electric	**Eastman Kodak**
	US Steel pfd	Goodrich	General Foods	**Exxon**
		Republic Iron & Steel	General Motors	**General Electric**
		Studebaker	Goodyear	**General Motors**
		Texas Company	IBM	**Goodyear**
		US Rubber	International Harvester	**IBM**
		US Steel	International Nickel	International Paper
		Utah Copper	International Shoe	McDonald's
		Westinghouse	Johns-Manville	Merck
		Western Union	Loew's	Minnesota Mining & Mfg
			Nash Motors	**Navistar (Intl Harvester)**

TABLE 2.1 The Dow Jones Index, 1896–1987 (continued)

1896	1905	1916	1932	1987
			Procter & Gamble	Philip Morris
			Sears Roebuck	**Procter & Gamble**
			Standard Oil CA (Chevron)	**Sears Roebuck**
			Standard Oil NJ (Exxon)	**Texaco**
			Texas Company (Texaco)	**Union Carbide**
			Union Carbide	United Technologies
			US Steel	**USX (US Steel)**
			Westinghouse	**Westinghouse**
			Woolworth	**Woolworth**

*Bold indicates corporations that have continued since 1932.

Source: "Dow Jones Industrial Average Historial Components," S&P Dow Jones Indices

ten mills each making 1,000 tons. The birth of mass production and eventually assembly lines extended scale economies to a wide range of manufactured goods. Combined with a national system of railroads, it became feasible to make much or most of the nation's steel in Pittsburgh, canned soup in Camden, cars in Detroit, soap in Cincinnati, tires in Akron, and so on.

Yet technology alone would not give us the giant organizations that spanned the 20th-century American economy. For that we needed advances in managerial technology, namely, the hierarchical organizational structures that allowed coordination of distinct and often dispersed operating units and control of the new industrial labor force. The giant steel mills, retail chains, and car factories could not run themselves—they needed management. Armies, railroads, and governments had experience with the traditional chain of command, but the emerging corporation refined it to a new level: After World War I, new schools of business provided a training ground for generations of professional managers to staff these new structures. This was, as Chandler put it, a managerial revolution. Corporations would be run not by families but by trained professionals.

Why the stock market mattered

WHAT THE NEW corporations had in common was size: Bigger was better, or at least more economical, in an increasing range of industries. Where the 19th-century American economy was largely agricultural and local, with every town having its own brewery and bakery, the 20th-century industrial economy was national in scope, thanks in large part to economies of scale. In this situation, the corporation emerged as the vessel to make it happen. The "economics of big" paved the way for the corporation.

Why did the new mass production and mass distribution organizations almost inevitably become public corporations, at least in the US?

The simplest answer is size. Vast scale does not normally come cheap, and enterprises large enough to serve a regional or national market often required very large fixed investments that were beyond the means of their founders or a small group of private investors. The railroads had demonstrated that the corporation was a reasonable structure to amass long-term capital from many investors and put it to work (although the industry was plagued with enough bankruptcies and scandal to scare off anyone who was paying attention).

There were alternatives, of course. In many countries, such as Germany, banks had the wherewithal to fund large-scale businesses. In others, such as France, the government funded and owned large businesses such as the railroads.

But politics, tradition, and scale made these options unlikely in the US. Until quite recently, banks in the US were tiny relative to the size of the national economy. Commercial banks (which take in deposits and make loans) were generally forbidden from operating across state lines until the early 1990s, and in many states (such as Iowa) they were prohibited from operating more than a single branch. At a time when Germany had three big universal banks, and Canadian banking was dominated by five national institutions, the US had thousands of local banks scattered across the country. Moreover, for generations commercial banks were prohibited from owning the stock of other corporations, which ruled out the possibility of German-style capitalism centered around a few large national banks.[5]

Government ownership of industry was also effectively out of the question. The US federal government was tiny relative to the size of the economy prior to World War I, and its component states liked it that way. American politics made significant government ownership essentially impossible, even for the railroads, where unfettered (and lightly regulated) competition among private firms had produced a system rife with inefficiencies and recurring financial distress. If the government did not own the railroads, it was hard to imagine that it would own the steel or sugar or automobile industries.

Finally, the American market—unlike anywhere else in the world—was the size of a continent, and still growing rapidly. The economical size for American firms was likely to be far larger than the economical size for, say, French or Italian firms. Capital would be required on a large scale for a long time, and providing capital was something that stock markets were good at.

Privately owned companies were not entirely wiped out by the corporation. Perhaps the most striking counterexample is the Ford Motor Company. Henry Ford's namesake company (actually his third venture) predated General Motors by several years. In an industry with dozens of competitors, Ford grew to dominance early on by pioneering a moving assembly line in 1913 that allowed a complete automobile to be put together in one plant, in Highland Park, Michigan. This new method drove down costs dramatically and allowed Ford to increase wages for workers—a necessity, given the boredom and unpleasantness of work on an assembly line.

Henry Ford's vision of vertically integrated production led to the creation of the famous River Rouge plant in Dearborn, Michigan, which was completed in 1927 and initially employed 75,000 workers.

The Rouge did not just assemble parts provided by suppliers but made its own steel, glass, fabrics, power, and cement, from supplies shipped on Ford-owned trains and ships, often from Ford-owned raw materials sources.[6] Ford even owned a rubber plantation in Brazil named Fordlandia.

Ford's mania for control extended to one other input: capital. The company was owned by Henry Ford and a few local investors until 1919, when Henry bought them out, and the company remained a family-owned business until its initial public offering on the New York Stock Exchange in 1956. To this day, the Ford family controls a class of stock with extra voting rights that essentially guarantees them control of the company.[7]

But Ford grew "organically" by selling more and more cars. Indeed, most of the company's growth until the late 1920s was dependent on only one product, the Model T, whose profits could finance further growth. In contrast, many of the largest corporations that emerged around the turn of the century were created by combining regional producers into national-scale businesses. Prior to the Sherman Antitrust Act of 1890, competitors in the same industry (such as railroads and oil) commonly sought to coordinate their businesses and limit price competition through "trusts" that oversaw certain parts of their activities while allowing them to otherwise operate independently. After 1890 trusts were illegal, yet outright combination was not. The result was a vast merger wave, particularly between 1898 and 1902, that was largely orchestrated by Wall Street firms such as J.P. Morgan. The wave crested with the 1901 merger of Carnegie Steel and many of its competitors and suppliers into US Steel, America's first billion-dollar corporation.

The corporate structure proved ideal for the new steel company. Participants in the merger could be paid in shares rather than cash, allowing the newly formed company to maintain its reserves for business activities. The shares could then be sold to third parties through the stock exchange, providing the investors with liquidity. Andrew Carnegie's share of the US Steel transaction was worth nearly a half billion dollars—enough to fund a nationwide building boom in public libraries and a host of other charitable activities. Exchange-listed corporations also held a great attraction for the bankers who organized them, including large fees, liquidity, and the prospect of ongoing control.[8]

Was concentration inevitable?

CONSIDER WHAT THE world looked like in early 1914.

In North America, Europe, and the Middle East, the previous century had seen political power grow to be concentrated in a handful of national governments. Europe enjoyed a century of relative peace after the end of the Napoleonic Wars in 1815. Italy and Germany had each become unified by 1871, merging countless tiny sovereigns into modern nation-states. The Austro-Hungarian Empire, the Russian Empire, and the Ottoman Empire controlled vast swaths of Europe, Asia, and the Middle East. European empires, particularly Great Britain and France, occupied large parts of Africa and Asia.

History's arrow seemed to point in one direction, toward ever-increasing political centralization overseen by a small but cordial community of nations (many of which were ruled by an extended set of cousins). New technologies and new industries, coupled with previously unknown levels of global trade, ensured rising standards of living for the foreseeable future—as long as there were no hiccups along the way.[9]

What was true of international politics was also true of the business world. In industry after industry, modest regional producers combined into large national and international players. In younger industries like automobiles, some new entrants like Ford rapidly grew into giant institutions. As Chandler pointed out in his historical analysis, by 1914 the American corporation already looked much the way it would for the rest of the century.

World War I abruptly ended the reign of several political empires, breaking them into their constituent parts (Poland, Turkey, Czechoslovakia, Iraq, Austria, and others). But for several decades more, corporations kept getting bigger and more encompassing, particularly in the US.

According to Adolf Berle and Gardiner Means, whose 1932 book *The Modern Corporation and Private Property* was the defining work on the modern corporation, "the economic power in the hands of the few persons who control a giant corporation is a tremendous force which can harm or benefit a multitude of individuals, affect whole districts, shift the currents of trade, bring ruin to one community and prosperity to another. The organizations which they control have passed far beyond the realm of private enterprise—they have become more nearly social institutions." As corporate control of assets became centripetal, or more concentrated and centralized over time, economies of scale seemed to have no horizon, with corporations continuing to grow larger and more encompassing and to employ an ever-larger part of the population. Giant corporations had replaced competitive capitalism with a new form of feudalism, with business executives occupying the role of princes. Thus, Berle and Means concluded with a prophecy:

> The modern corporation may be regarded not simply as one form of social organization but potentially (if not yet actually) as the dominant institution of the modern world. . . . The rise of the modern corporation has brought a concentration of economic power which can compete on equal terms with the modern state—economic power versus political power, each strong in its own field. . . . The future may see the economic organism, now typified by the corporation, not only on an equal plane with the state, but possibly even superseding it as the dominant form of social organization.[10]

Why exactly corporations seemed to grow without limit was unclear, but whatever the cause, Berle and Means' prediction was prescient. For a half-century after their book was published, corporations continued to grow larger and more concentrated and to shape not just the American economy, but society itself.

What the corporation wrought

IN THE OPENING of her essay "Mr. Bennett and Mrs. Brown," Virginia Woolf made a striking claim: "On or about December 1910, human character changed." She went on: "All human relations have shifted— those between masters and servants, husbands and wives, parents and children. And when human relations change there is at the same time a change in religion, conduct, politics and literature."[11]

Looking back, it is clear that Woolf was right: Massive changes were taking place in the culture and society of the West. Einstein published his special theory of relativity in 1905. William James published his lectures on pragmatism in 1907, the same year Picasso painted *Les Demoiselles d'Avignon*. Stravinsky premiered *The Rite of Spring* in 1913, the year of the famous Armory Show at the International Exhibition of Modern Art and the publication of *Swann's Way* by Marcel Proust. Science, philosophy, art, music, and literature were taking a modernist turn on the verge of World War I.[12]

The economy was also undergoing massive shifts, with the transition from agriculture to manufacturing and the movement of people from country to city. New industries were being created left and right: movies, automobiles, airplanes, and all the household products enabled by electrification. Was it just a coincidence that corporations arose at the same time as these other social changes?

Later writers would see corporations having a massive cultural influence. In 1949 management theorist Peter Drucker claimed that the industrial corporation "determines the individual's view of his society," even among those who did not work there. The way that corporations did things—particularly mass production—became the way that things were done, from how farms were run to how schools taught students to how countries waged war. "The big enterprise is the true symbol of our social order . . . . In the industrial enterprise the structure which actually underlies all our society can be seen."[13]

Corporations were a force that could reshape society. In the next chapter, we consider how society tried to channel this force.

CHAPTER 3

TAMING THE CORPORATION

THE EMERGENCE OF the large corporation in the early 20th century created a dilemma. On the one hand, corporations were an efficient way to organize an industrial economy. They invented new goods and services and provided them on a large scale. They created jobs for millions of people, and moved America from an agricultural and rural economy to an urban manufacturing economy. On the other hand, those who controlled corporations wielded vast economic power. Corporations seemed to grow bigger and more concentrated year by year, giving them the potential to dominate politics as well as the economy. What was to prevent them from creating an industrial oligarchy?

Throughout American history, its citizens have resisted the concentration and centralization of power, both economic and political. This resistance can be seen in the rise of the Tea Party in American politics, which is the most recent of a long line of movements that favored power remaining with individual states, rather than concentrated in a large federal government. Yet while the rise of corporations brought the promise of abundance, it also brought the threat of concentrated power.

In this chapter, I describe how the United States addressed this dilemma. Ironically, the solution to the problems created by concentrated economic power was concentrated political power. Powerful national corporations would be reined in by a powerful national government.

Power in the corporate economy

IN A BRIEF period at the turn of the 20th century, a new and unfamiliar corporate economy emerged in the US. Dozens of mergers brokered by Wall Street bankers led to the creation of a new corporatized economy, with many industries dominated by just a few large players. A nation of competitive regional economies turned into an oligopolistic national economy. America had little prior experience with these imposing new organisms. The most substantial corporations in the 19th century had been railroads. Now corporations increasingly dominated the manufacturing and service economy as well. What were citizens to do about the giant new steel company, or the giant new telephone company, or the giant new retail chains? Who would control them, and what goals would they serve? This question animated the Progressive movement in the early decades of the century.

The US had a long history of resistance to concentrated power. The federal system of government gave the individual states great power to control their own local economies. Corporations were chartered by states, not the national government, and although banks could hold state or national charters after the Civil War, they still operated by rules at the state level. Both political and economic power in the US had been spread among the states. When economic power threatened to become concentrated, as in the railroad and oil industries, political forces reined it in. But now corporations dominated many industries, and threatened to dominate politics at the national level.

At the time of the "corporate revolution," the US federal government was no match for the new corporations. Federal government revenues in 1910 were less than $900 million, and derived largely from customs and taxes on alcohol and tobacco. There was no federal income tax, no Federal Reserve Bank, no Department of Labor. Meanwhile, US Steel's assets topped $1.3 billion. The corporate sector was now huge and national in scope, with the potential to form a powerful new ruling class that could dominate government.

Taming the banks

FOR MOST OF American history, its banks have been much smaller and more limited than those of other countries. In most industrial economies, banks operate on a national and often international level. "Banks" can take in deposits, make loans, underwrite securities, and perhaps write insurance policies and sell mutual funds. The traditional "universal bank" was a one-stop shop for almost anything having to do with finance. And because many of the things banks do had economies of scale, just like manufacturing, many countries came to have a few dominant national banks. Yet this consolidation did not happen in the US until the end of the 20th century.

Fear of financial power, and particularly the unseen operations of banks, runs deep in American history. In a famous scene in *The Grapes of Wrath*, John Steinbeck writes "The bank is something else than men. It happens that every man in a bank hates what the bank does, and yet the bank does it. The bank is something more than men, I tell you. It's the monster. Men made it, but they can't control it." He then describes a tenant farmer who is being evicted confronting a man on a tractor about to destroy his house. The man on the tractor tries to reason with the farmer and his gun:

> "It's not me. There's nothing I can do. I'll lose my job if I don't do it. And look—suppose you kill me? They'll just hang you, but long before you're hung there'll be another guy on the tractor, and he'll bump the house down. You're not killing the right guy."
>
> "That's so," the tenant said. "Who gave you orders? I'll go after him. He's the one to kill."
>
> "You're wrong. He got his orders from the bank. The bank told him, 'Clear those people out or it's your job.'"
>
> "Well, there's a president of the bank. There's a board of directors. I'll fill up the magazine of the rifle and go into the bank."

The driver said, "Fellow was telling me the bank gets orders from the East. The orders were, 'Make the land show profit or we'll close you up.'"

"But where does it stop? Who can we shoot? I don't aim to starve to death before I kill the man that's starving me."

"I don't know. Maybe there's nobody to shoot. Maybe the thing isn't men at all."[1]

While the founding fathers were divided on the question of what kinds of banks the new nation would have, Andrew Jackson set the tone for the rest of the 19th century when he vetoed a bill rechartering the Second Bank of the United States in 1832. The bank had an effective monopoly on the federal government's business, and was structured in a way that lent itself to dominance by a few investors. "There is danger that a [bank] president and directors would then be able to elect themselves from year to year, and without responsibility or control manage the whole concerns of the bank during the existence of its charter. It is easy to conceive that great evils to our country and its institutions millet flow from such a concentration of power in the hands of a few men irresponsible to the people."[2] If threatened, they might use their power to sway elections or "control the affairs of the nation."

Jackson concluded that the government should not aid the rich by giving them control of a powerful bank:

It is to be regretted that the rich and powerful too often bend the acts of government to their selfish purposes. Distinctions in society will always exist under every just government. Equality of talents, of education, or of wealth can not be produced by human institutions. . . . But when the laws undertake to add to these natural and just advantages artificial distinctions, to grant titles, gratuities, and exclusive privileges, to make the rich richer and the potent more powerful, the humble members of society—the farmers, mechanics, and laborers—who have neither the time nor the means of securing like favors to themselves, have a right to complain of the injustice of their Government.

For the next 150 years, American banks were fragmented both in what they could do and where they could operate. The US had different banks for lending to business (commercial banks), lending to home buyers (savings and loans), making smaller personal loans (credit unions), underwriting stocks and bonds (investment banks)—all facing different customers and different regulators, some at the state level and some at the national level. More peculiarly, until the early 1990s commercial banks were generally limited to operating branches within only a single state, and each state had its own rules. For instance, an Indiana bank could not open an office in Illinois. As a result, by 1980 the US had over 12,000 commercial banking organizations spread across the country, while Canadian banking was dominated by just five major national banks.[3] Banks in the US remained relatively small and local when those in the rest of the world had become big and global.

The emergence of the corporate economy in the early 20th century created a new potential for concentrated economic control, and for bankers to again exercise undue influence. Louis Brandeis, a future Supreme Court justice, laid out the case against the banks in a series of articles published in *Harper's Magazine* in 1913 and subsequently compiled into 1914's *Other People's Money: And How the Bankers Use It*. Bankers in New York had created the new corporations by organizing mergers among regional companies, and now they maintained a hand in their operation by placing representatives on their boards. Here, Brandeis named names: J.P. Morgan and his eponymous firm, James Stillman of National City, George F. Baker of First National. (Some of Brandeis's culprits will sound familiar to those who have visited Harvard Business School's campus and the buildings bearing their names.) Baker himself served on 22 corporate boards, Stillman and his colleagues served on 48 boards, and J.P. Morgan partners held "72 directorships in 47 of the largest corporations of the country."

J.P. Morgan had organized General Electric, International Harvester, US Steel, and many more of the new giants, and he and his partners continued to serve on their boards, where they could control firms through their chokehold on the supply of new capital. Brandeis further called attention to the possibilities for collusion enabled by the "endless chain" of companies that shared directors. Industry had become organized into oligopolies, often with two to three leading firms (e.g., GE and Westinghouse; US Steel and Bethlehem Steel), and in many cases partners from the same bank served on the boards of all the major competitors. What better way to evade antitrust restrictions than to have the same people serving on the boards of competitors?[4]

Yet the threat of financial institutions controlling the industrial economy faded almost as soon as the ink was dry on Brandeis's book. The Clayton Act, enacted in October 1914, banned directors serving on the boards of firms in the same industry. With a few exceptions, bankers resigned their board seats en masse in 1914 on the verge of World War I.[5] During the war, retail brokerages opened to sell war bonds to the public, and subsequently created a beachhead for selling corporate shares to Main Street. Thus, the number of shareholders in the US doubled between 1924 and 1927, and doubled again by 1930.[6] As a result of this flood of new investors into the stock market, ownership in the typical corporation had become highly dispersed by 1930, and the threat of direct control of corporations by bankers faded. Indeed, the broad dispersion of shareholdings raised the question of whether anyone was still in charge. Meanwhile, banks were blamed for the stock market crash that kicked off the Great Depression, and the Glass-Steagall Act of 1933 created a legal wall between investment banking and commercial banking that endured for over six decades. Banks had been effectively tamed.

Taming the corporations

CORPORATIONS WERE ANOTHER story. After the breakup of Standard Oil in 1911 (which created the companies that evolved into Exxon, Mobil, Chevron, Amoco, Marathon, and several others), industrial corporations were left to grow as big as they could, within certain constraints. Given the vast size and growth of the American economy, few industries ended up being dominated by true monopolists. Rather, many industries had a Big Three or Big Four. New industries were being created, enabled by new technologies: autos and trucks, home appliances, film, radio broadcasting, discount retailing, pharmaceuticals, and more. During the 1920s, another wave of mergers further consolidated these new industries, often through vertical integration. The result was a set of dominant firms that held sway for the next half century.[7]

In their 1932 book *The Modern Corporation and Private Property*, Adolf Berle and Gardiner Means charted the growth of American corporations in the two decades after Brandeis's essays. They found that economic power had become increasingly concentrated in a few dozen corporations, as if a "centripetal force" were operating. The 200 biggest nonfinancial corporations controlled 49.2% of corporate wealth by 1929, and if the trends of the previous decade continued, they would control it all by 1959.

What was to be done in the face of this staggering new power? Theodore Roosevelt had addressed this question in a speech to Civil War veterans in Osawatomie, Kansas, in 1910. In some sense, the growth of large corporations reflected economies of scale, as we described in the first chapter. If bigger was cheaper, then corporate growth seemed almost inevitable. Manufacturing firms in the 1800s were limited in size by the wealth of their immediate owners. But corporations listed on stock markets faced no such limits, and could grow without restraint. Antitrust laws alone were doomed to fail because economies of scale meant that busting up large firms would reduce efficiency. As Roosevelt put it, "Combinations in industry are the result of an imperative economic law which cannot be repealed by political legislation. The effort at prohibiting all combinations has substantially failed. The way out lies, not in attempting to prevent such combinations, but in completely controlling them in the interest of public welfare."[8]

The charge, then, was to find the means to harness corporations to serve the public good. And that would require a far larger central government than Americans were used to.

Growing the government

ROOSEVELT'S "NEW NATIONALISM" speech laid out a program for progressivism for the next several decades. His diagnosis of the problem was clear. Wealth was becoming increasingly concentrated due to the growth of the new corporations, and the wealthy were using their resources to corrupt politics. The problem was not wealth per se, but how it was gained, and how it was used. "We grudge no man a fortune in civil life if it is honorably obtained and well used. It is not even enough that it should have been gained without doing damage to the community. We should permit it to be gained only so long as the gaining represents benefit to the community."

The single biggest threat came from the "sinister influence" of special interests, and specifically the new corporations. "The citizens of the United States must effectively control the mighty commercial forces which they have called into being . . . . It is necessary that laws should be passed to prohibit the use of corporate funds directly or indirectly for political purposes . . . [to avoid] corruption in our political affairs."

At the time that Roosevelt spoke, the federal government was miniscule. The Food and Drug Administration was only 4 years old. There was no Department of Labor or Federal Reserve. There was no income tax. Familiar features of government that we take for granted did not exist and had to be invented—in large part to tame the new corporations.

In order to guide the economic forces that the corporation had unleashed toward public benefit, Roosevelt proposed an agenda that was largely realized in subsequent years. "The absence of effective State, and, especially, national, restraint upon unfair money-getting has tended to create a small class of enormously wealthy and economically powerful men, whose chief object is to hold and increase their power." To take on this problem "implies a policy of a far more active governmental interference with social and economic conditions in this country than we have yet had, but I think we have got to face the fact that such an increase in governmental control is now necessary." In short, we would need a far larger and more intrusive federal government that took a direct hand in regulating the corporate economy.

How would this new mandate be funded? By a steeply progressive income tax and a stiff inheritance tax to prevent the accumulation of dynastic fortunes—"properly safeguarded against evasion, and increasing rapidly in amount with the size of the estate." After all, "the essence of any struggle for healthy liberty has always been, and must always be, to take from some one man or class of men the right to enjoy power, or wealth, or position, or immunity, which has not been earned by service to his or their fellows."

During subsequent years, government employment grew rapidly, along with a proliferation of new departments and agencies. To a large extent, the growth of the corporation prompted the growth of government.

Americans had let loose a powerful new force with the potential to create enormous economic growth and prosperity, yet it also needed a powerful counterweight to prevent it from dominating politics and society. A struggle was thus born between big business and big government that lasted for decades.

CHAPTER 4

THE POSTWAR ERA
OF CORPORATE DOMINANCE

CORPORATIONS CONTINUED TO grow larger and more concentrated for most of the 20th century. The mobilization for World War II created massive growth in employment in manufacturing. It also spread standardized personnel practices across industry and encouraged companies to adopt policies to attract and retain workers, including health benefits and retirement pensions. After the war, big unionized firms in autos and steel created a set of social welfare benefits such as health care for workers and their families, wage stability in the event of layoffs, and retirement pensions that ended up becoming a model for other employers. The benefits that governments provided to citizens in Europe and Canada became the responsibility of corporate employers for American citizens.

The postwar economic boom corresponded to three decades of corporate dominance. Corporations kept getting bigger and more concentrated in assets and employment, reaching a pinnacle around 1970, when two dozen corporations employed nearly 10% of the labor force. At the same time, income inequality reached its lowest level in American history. An entry-level job at a growing corporation provided a straight path to the middle class and growing prosperity. Paradoxically, hierarchical corporations seemed to reduce inequality and provide a form of economic security.

As corporations enveloped more of people's economic lives, the federal government increasingly used them as tools to implement policy. Richard Nixon presided over a massive expansion in government regulation of the corporate economy, from the EPA (Environmental Protection Agency) and OSHA (Occupational Safety and Health Administration) to the EEOC (Equal Employment Opportunity Commission) and wage/price controls. During subsequent years, the economy slid into a malaise of inflation and low growth, and the stock market began to punish the giant conglomerates that had built up during previous decades.

All this set the stage for a revenge of the shareholders, described in the next chapter.

The adolescence of the corporate sector

BY 1930 THE American corporate economy was fully grown. As Berle and Means discovered, a mere 200 companies controlled half of non-financial corporate assets. The vast majority of manufacturing workers were employed in corporations. The familiar names of the corporate century were now well established: AT&T, DuPont, Eastman Kodak, General Electric, General Motors, Sears, Westinghouse, Woolworth. Most companies listed in the Dow Jones Index in 1930 were still there 60 years later. Corporate stability had taken hold.

Prior to the Depression-era reforms, labor stability remained elusive. Employee strife was common among large manufacturers, and the right to organize was contested, often brutally. The National Labor Relations Act ("Wagner Act") of 1935 guaranteed workers the right to form unions and bargain collectively, and by the time of America's entry into World War II, major manufacturing industries had been organized, albeit often after violent struggle. The Social Security Act, also passed in 1935, created a basic safety net for workers and their dependents, including modest old age pensions and benefits for the unemployed.

World War II greatly expanded corporate employment and made the corporation far more bureaucratic. In 1944, the percentage of employment in manufacturing in the United States reached its highest level. The "Arsenal of Democracy," as Franklin D. Roosevelt referred to our collective efforts during the war, turned into a jobs machine and helped induce a wave of migration north. Ford's River Rouge plant came to employ over 100,000 people within a single gigantic complex in Dearborn, Michigan. GM's employment more than doubled from 220,000 in 1939 to 464,000 in 1944, at the height of wartime production.[1]

At the same time, the federal government took on an unprecedented level of control, from a freeze on wages to the encouragement of shared industry employment practices designed to limit employee turnover. Many companies created centralized personnel departments and systems of job evaluation in order to document their labor needs in a newly regulated market, and adopted employment practices designed to maintain long-term ties to their employees, such as formalized job ladders. Many of these new bureaucratic controls remained in place long after the war was over. Across the economy, companies became more bureaucratic, more regimented, and more similar to each other.[2]

The "Treaty of Detroit" and the era of corporate benevolence

THE END OF the war created a great deal of uncertainty. The victory over fascism was a triumph for democracy, but what would happen to the economy when all the troops shed their uniforms and headed back to the civilian economy, and the government ended its de facto stimulus program? It seemed entirely possible that the US would return to an economic depression marked by high unemployment, this time saddled with an unprecedented national debt to pay off.

Things turned out otherwise. The GI Bill provided a wide range of government services to returning veterans, including low-cost mortgages (which helped spark a construction boom) and education subsidies (which sent over 2 million vets to college). Moreover, the war had pent up consumer demand for years, and now there was an opportunity to finally buy new homes, new cars, and new appliances.

With prosperity came new demands from labor. The war had frozen wages, and now it was time to catch up. One particular labor agreement turned out to be a landmark in reshaping the corporation. In late 1945 and early 1946, the United Auto Workers organized a nationwide strike against GM that lasted for months. The UAW strike took place as part of the largest wave of strikes in American history, with the steel, oil, and electrical industries also impacted. These strikes and the labor agreements that resulted from them, shaped the postwar environment for labor relations. During the 1949 negotiations with GM, the UAW had grander ambitions than merely increased wages: Employers would take on the provision of health and welfare services, including retirement pensions. The resulting agreement, known as the "Treaty of Detroit," provided covered workers with a reasonably generous company-paid pension upon retirement as well as coverage for medical care for workers and their families. The plan was quickly adopted by the other major automakers and then spread widely throughout industry.[3]

The Treaty of Detroit effectively created a new understanding of the employment relation: Employers were now expected to provide health and retirement benefits, not just for their top executives, but for all employees. This was unique. In the rest of the industrialized world, governments took on health insurance and retirement security. The United Kingdom and Canada created nationalized health care systems that provided coverage as a basic benefit of citizenship. In the US, however, these were now the job of the corporation. From that point forward, corporate employers became a predominant source of social welfare services in the United States.

In retrospect, it is clear what might go wrong with this system. Many employers ultimately abandoned "defined benefit" pension plans; others altered the terms of their health plans. GM itself canceled its health coverage for white-collar retirees in the mid-2000s and turned over health insurance for unionized workers to a trust fund. But at the time, the agreement had an irresistible appeal. It is much easier to offer workers a higher pension, to be paid down the road, than to increase wages today. Promises made at the bargaining table now will be kept (or not) on someone else's watch, years in the future.

Prosperity, equality, mobility, and security

THE POSTWAR ERA of corporate dominance corresponded to a period of remarkable economic growth, social mobility, and relative income equality in the United States. Gross domestic product (GDP), productivity, and household income grew at a remarkable rate during this period, which is now widely regarded as a golden era for the American economy. It was not just in the US: The period from 1945 to 1975 is called the "glorious thirty" ("les trente glorieuses") in France, and both Western Europe and East Asia saw similar periods of growing prosperity. But in the US this era is distinctively associated with the corporate economy.

Corporations grew increasingly large and concentrated in assets and employment. Berle and Means's forecast that 200 corporations would control the economy by 1959 turned out to be not entirely accurate, but they got the direction right. Large corporations grew ever larger during the 30 years after World War II (see Figure 4.1), and by 1973 the 25 largest corporations employed the equivalent of nearly 10% of the labor force.[4] Not all firms grew like this, but enough did to feed a narrative of endless growth. Some of this was "organic" growth: As the population grew and dispersed to suburbs, demand for telephone service, cars, and retail also grew. But many firms grew through relentless acquisitions. Although antitrust concerns limited the ability of firms to grow by acquiring competitors or suppliers, many companies like ITT grew by diversifying into any industry where they saw opportunity.

At the same time, income inequality dropped to its lowest recorded level in American history, while upward mobility increased. Statistics on household income show that the late 1960s was when the US reached its lowest recorded level of income inequality. Certainly, the US had not turned into Denmark—or even Canada, for that matter—but incomes were more evenly distributed around 1968 than

FIGURE 4.1 Employment of selected US corporations in thousands, 1950–73

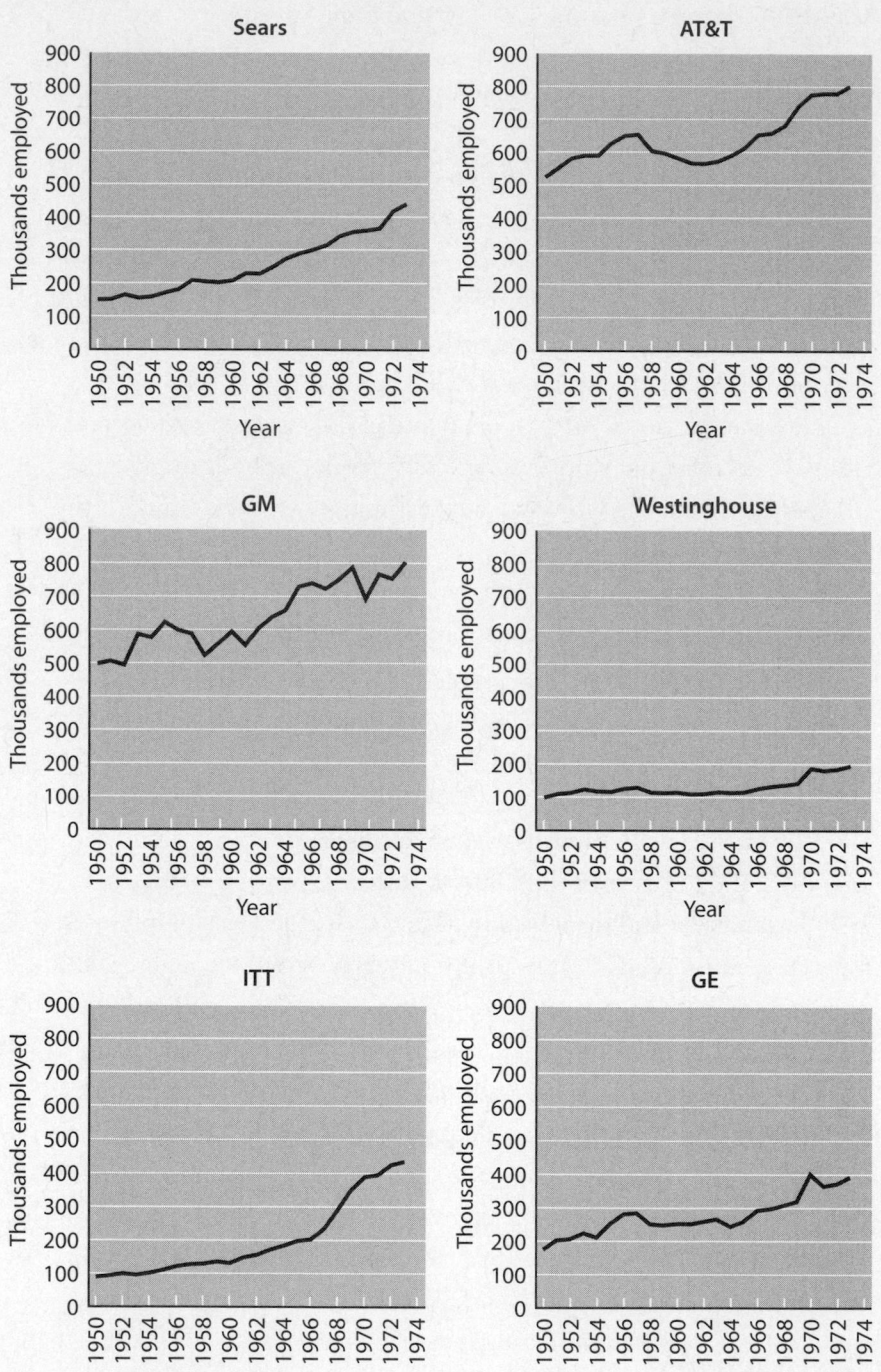

Source: Compustat

they ever were before or since (a theme discussed in more detail in Chapter 10).

It was also a period of employment opportunity. Growing firms with clear job ladders provided a straightforward path to mobility. An entry-level job with a major corporation that had a strong commitment to promotion from within was a ticket to the middle class. Rewards based on seniority, including the pensions and retiree health insurance that grew out of the Treaty of Detroit, made a corporate career a safe bet.

It seems paradoxical to see large corporations as sources of greater equality. What could be more unequal than a giant corporation, with its pyramid-shaped organization chart and executive washrooms? The whole point of "job ladders" is that corporations are full of hierarchical levels to climb up, and endless contests for status. Yet corporations, with their detailed job descriptions, career ladders, and seniority systems, also managed to limit and rationalize inequality through their centralized personnel systems. Promotion from within meant that salaries were determined not so much by the outside market but by standardized evaluations for what a job was worth.

Consider ITT, the poster child conglomerate that grew through a voracious series of acquisitions in every industry you could name: hotels, casinos, auto parts manufacturers, copper mines, insurance companies, trade schools, bakeries, and more. When it acquired a new company, it sent in its people to impose ITT's personnel system, spreading the ITT way to dozens of industries. The personnel management systems that spread during the war became more standardized and covered ever more employees. Shielded from market processes, jobs and compensation systems followed bureaucratic rules that limited just how unequal they could get.[5]

The corporation as a lever of social policy

PERHAPS NO PRESIDENT in history fulfilled Teddy Roosevelt's progressive vision more effectively than Richard Nixon. During Nixon's time as president, at the height of corporate concentration and power, the federal government greatly expanded its control over what corporations did. Indeed, some of the regulators most hated by big business were created during Nixon's first term. The Environmental Protection Agency was born in 1970, regulating corporate polluters and mandating gas mileage increases. Nixon signed the bill creating the Occupational Safety and Health Administration that same year, further expanding the government's reach into private employment practices. In 1972 the Equal Employment Opportunity Commission got litigation authority, and promptly used it to pursue investigations of discrimination in four of America's largest employers (Sears, GM, GE, and Ford).[6]

Nixon also sought a more progressive tax system. His signing statement for the Tax Reform Act of 1969 states:

> More than 9 million low-income people who pay taxes will be dropped from the tax rolls. This results primarily from the special low-income allowance that I proposed last April as a means of making sure that people at or below the poverty level do not have to pay Federal income taxes. . . . A large number of high-income persons who have paid little or no Federal income taxes will now bear a fairer share of the tax burden through enactment of a minimum income tax comparable to the proposal that I submitted to the Congress, which closes the loopholes that permitted much of this tax avoidance . . . . Congress also accepted this administration's recommendation to increase Social Security payments, enabling our older citizens to maintain their standard of living in the face of rising prices.[7]

It is hard to imagine any contemporary president pursuing such an overtly progressive agenda. But at the time, corporations had become so vast and encompassing that any effort at social reform had to use corporations as tools. They were the major polluters, and the major source of hope for conservation. They were the largest employers, and therefore the place to implement efforts at worker safety and equality of opportunity. Changing the hiring and promotion practices of two-dozen corporate employers to be more equitable could substantially change the lives of one-tenth of the nation's workforce. And if the previous three decades' experience was any guide, corporations would continue to get even bigger and even more powerful. A wit at the time suggested that if trends in consolidation continued, *Fortune* magazine would have to change the title of the Fortune 500 list because there would not be enough independent companies left to fill it.

Conglomerates and emerging cracks in corporate dominance

BUT 1973 WAS a turning point. The Organization of Petroleum Exporting Countries (OPEC) declared an oil embargo in October that quadrupled oil prices within a few months. Meanwhile, a severe recession set in that marked the end of the postwar boom, and economic growth lagged for much of the decade, while inflation accelerated. The economic conditions that had supported the postwar boom had largely evaporated.

In spite of this, corporations continued to seek growth wherever they could. The conglomerate mergers pioneered by ITT and others of its ilk spread broadly across the corporate sector. What was initially a novelty became standard practice. The question of what industry a company belonged in was hard to answer in many cases, as the diversified conglomerate became the modal type of corporation in the US. Endless acquisitions seemed like a sure path to growth, but it was not without a cost. By 1980, conglomerates were chronically undervalued by the stock market: A big company that operated in five industries was often worth less than five small companies would be worth as a group.[8] But big was beautiful, and there was no easy way to split these companies back up into portfolios; their hypothetical value was of mostly academic interest.

All this would change, however, with the presidential election of 1980.

WHY THE AMERICAN CORPORATION IS DISAPPEARING

PART II

WHY THE AMERICAN CORPORATION IS DISAPPEARING

Fᴏʀ ᴍᴏsᴛ ᴏғ the 20th century, American corporations sought growth. This often meant merging with competitors or, after World War II, acquiring companies in unrelated industries. The conglomerate merger movement of the 1960s left the biggest firms highly diversified. ITT became one of the biggest corporations in the world by buying insurance companies, bakeries, auto suppliers, hotel chains, trade schools, copper mines, and hundreds of other businesses. But the pursuit of sales growth often came at the expense of shareholders, who preferred profitability. Ronald Reagan's election in 1980 changed the rules for how corporations could and should operate. The hostile takeover wave of the 1980s, activist investors, and the growth of stock ownership by the broad public ushered in an era of shareholder value dominance. This represented a major shift in how scholars and the public thought about the corporation and its responsibilities, and brought about substantial changes in how corporations were managed. Where corporations in the postwar era aimed to balance the interests of many stakeholders, by the end of the 1980s shareholders had emerged as the corporation's dominant constituency.

The outsourcing movement of the 1990s metastasized into a broad hollowing-out of the American corporation. Following a model popularized by Nike, American corporations increasingly hived off the production and distribution of their goods and services to focus on the higher value-added tasks of design and marketing. Surprisingly few goods are actually produced by the company whose brand is on the label, from iPhones to cat food to blood thinner. The result has been disastrous for American employment, even in "high-growth" industries such as electronics. It has also resulted in a conundrum about "corporate responsibility," as supply chains are increasingly dispersed around the world and illegible even to the companies owning the brand. Few sectors are immune, whether in manufacturing or service.

The growth of generic manufacturers and distributors and the widespread availability of cloud services mean that barriers to entry have collapsed in many industries. Anyone with a credit card and a Web connection can create an enterprise, from incorporation to production to distribution. The economies of scale that gave birth to the modern corporation have disappeared in many sectors. Lightweight entrants can scale up or down rapidly by renting rather than buying capacity, and their low cost means that in many domains they are a superior choice. These lightweight firms with modest time horizons have little rationale for bearing the costs of going public. Meanwhile, incumbent firms face existential threats requiring substantial and uncertain restructuring, which often requires exiting the stock market. The decline of the public corporation does not mean that business *per se* is collapsing. There are many ways to organize enterprises, legally and financially, and the current era has seen a flowering of alternative forms. Thanks to low barriers to entry, new ways of organizing business are emerging almost daily.

The range of activities for which the most economical format is to organize as a corporation and sell shares to the public is rapidly diminishing. Firms that have gone public since the dot-com collapse of 2000 often flout standards of corporate governance (e.g., by giving founders permanent control via super-voting shares). Their rationale for going public—to pay off employees and early investors, rather than to raise capital to invest in long-lived assets—suggests that such firms are not sustainable as public companies for the long term, although demand for returns by investors may sustain them for some time.

CHAPTER 5

SHAREHOLDERS GET
THE UPPER HAND

B Y THE 1970s, American corporations had reached their peak in size
and economic dominance. ITT and its ilk had shown that companies were not limited to a single industry: Under the banner of "synergy," conglomerates bought smaller businesses in whatever industry
seemed promising. The strategy of diversification spread to nearly every
major corporation, and the very idea of being in a single industry came
to seem outdated. Yet shareholders had good reason to hate conglomerates, as they were frequently worth less than the sum of their parts.
An economy-wide spree of acquisitions in the 1960s and '70s had left
the corporate sector bloated, incoherent, and undervalued. The "blue
chips" were like a high school football team at their thirtieth class
reunion: once mighty but now gone to seed.

   After the election of Ronald Reagan in 1980, shareholders had a
chance to claim the value that had been locked up in the conglomerates. Antitrust regulators came to believe that industry concentration
was not always bad for consumers and loosened the rules against horizontal mergers, and the courts swept away laws that made hostile takeovers difficult. As a result, in under a decade nearly one-third of the
Fortune 500 merged or were acquired, most commonly through hostile
takeovers that often led to conglomerates being broken into parts
and sold off to industry competitors. Although shareholders benefited
handsomely from takeovers, employees and communities generally
did not, as takeover targets were often "streamlined." Takeover battles
brought new urgency to the question of who the corporation was for,

and where its obligations lay. But by the early 1990s, a clear answer had emerged: The corporation existed to create shareholder value.

The consensus around shareholder value had a lot of reinforcement. Executive compensation came to be overwhelmingly tied to share price, through the award of stock options and other forms of stock-based pay. The broader public also became heavily invested in the stock market. Beginning in 1982 and accelerating afterwards, companies shifted workers from traditional pension plans (which paid them a guaranteed income in retirement if they stayed with the company) to portable 401(k) plans invested in stock mutual funds. By 2000, most American households had some of their savings in the stock market, mutual funds had grown massive, and financial media were pervasive. Both executives and the middle class had reasons to follow the movements of the market, and to favor market-friendly policies. Meanwhile, shareholder activists had honed their skills at enforcing the gospel of shareholder value, while other corporate stakeholders had lost standing. By the turn of the new century, in the eyes of the most powerful constituencies, corporations existed to create shareholder value.

The problem with conglomerates

THE 1970s WAS in some sense the high-water mark of the American corporation. Driven by an imperative for growth, and urged on by consultants sharing visions of boundless synergies, Fortune 500 companies had grown vast through acquisitions. The idea that companies operated in an "industry" had come to seem increasingly archaic. Westinghouse Electric, a nearly century-old manufacturer of heavy electric equipment and appliances, also bottled soda; managed real estate; developed curricula for schools (including my own high school); produced wristwatches, locomotives, office furniture, semiconductors, air conditioners, escalators, and controls for nuclear weapons; operated radio and television stations; and controlled a substantial financial subsidiary, just like its ancient rival General

Electric. Beatrice, nominally a packaged food company making brands like La Choy, also owned Culligan plumbing supplies, Airstream travel trailers, Harman Kardon audio equipment, Samsonite luggage, and many others.[1]

Conglomerates demonstrated that talented senior executives could manage anything, in any and every industry. ITT (originally "International Telephone & Telegraph") owned major businesses around the world in insurance, auto parts, baked goods, hotels, copper mining, vocational education, auto rentals, telecommunications, and more. An outsider might imagine that this portfolio was chosen at random, but its visionary CEO, Harold Geneen, insisted that there was a method at work: "An 'operating conglomerate' is a centrally managed company that gets deep into each of its operations. . . . Its job is to own and operate companies—ideally through its strong, centralized management."[2] With the right people in charge, there was no limit to growth.

"Conglomerate" sounds like a distinctive type of organization, but by the late 1970s, almost all major corporations in the United States were diversified, trading in and out of industries on a regular basis. My grandfather, who worked as a welder for Ford Motor Company from 1919 until his retirement almost five decades later, was able to furnish his house in Dearborn with radios, a television, and a refrigerator all made by Ford Philco, and could finance them with Ford credit and drive them home in his Ford car.

Judged by their size, American corporations had never been more successful. Yet the American economy was suffering from an unprecedented malaise. After 25 years of economic growth, the dismal economy of the 1970s was something of a shock. Starting with the oil crisis of 1973, the decade witnessed several years of high inflation, low growth, and persistent unemployment, which came to be called "stag-flation." It was as if the engine of corporate capitalism had somehow seized up.

American corporations also found themselves facing unprecedented foreign competition, particularly from the revived manufacturing powerhouses of Japan and Germany. It was easy for American corporations to win against the devastated economies of Europe and Asia in the years after World War II, but this had arguably led them to pay less attention to quality and cost. In a reglobalized world economy, however, quality mattered, as even American consumers came to appreciate the virtues of Toyota and Honda.

Some saw a link between the triumph of gigantic corporations and economic malaise. Size and industrial diversity were the enemy of nimbleness. According to *The Economist* in 1992, "Corporate America's sluggish response to oil crises, Japanese competition, and other changes had much to do with its conglomerate tangles of the 1960s." If you can buy your way to growth, why bother with quality? And in any case, even if customers were not always delighted with their products, big and growing companies provided security and opportunity for employees. Major American corporations provided the kind of job security and career mobility that only the civil service could vouchsafe elsewhere in the world.

One constituency that conglomerates were clearly failing was shareholders. Inflation was high and stock market returns were weak for most of the 1970s. Diversified firms were among the worst offenders: Their tactic of growth through acquisition often lacked any clear rationale beyond the magical thinking of consultants. The idea that good management could manage anything seemed implausible on its face. Moreover, their stock was systematically undervalued relative to focused companies in the same industries, making the whole worth less than the sum of the parts, which was known as the "conglomerate discount." Companies like ITT, Beatrice, or Westinghouse had negative synergies. One Wall Street firm created a valuation model to predict what a conglomerate would be worth if it were split up. Its name? "Chop shop," in honor of the garages that took stolen cars and disassembled them into their parts for resale. Its creators noted a simple but powerful truth about conglomerates: "The more divisions a company has, the more likely it is to be undervalued."[3]

The Reagan revolution and the rise of the hostile takeover

THE ELECTION OF Ronald Reagan resulted in massive changes in economic policy and regulation, much of it guided by the work of academics who wanted to bring economic thinking to analysis of the law. This new thinking also set the stage for the wholesale dismantling of the conglomerate. Scholars in the "law and economics" movement were prone to seeing markets in places that others did not see them, and to attributing powers to markets that were also imperceptible to nonbelievers.

Henry G. Manne at the University of Chicago was a pioneer in this world. For decades commentators had assumed that dispersed shareholders had little influence over the corporations they nominally owned—that's why their managers chose growth over profitability. Manne, however, argued that the stock market played a critical disciplinary role. First, a company's stock price provided a minute-by-minute report card on how well management was doing, because stock markets provided the best available indicator of the company's expected future profitability (an idea then being formalized as the "efficient market hypothesis"). Second, if a company's stock price fell low enough, there was money to be made by outsiders—so-called "raiders"—to buy up shares of the company on the stock market, fire the people in charge, and rehabilitate the business for a profit. He described this as one of the great get-rich-quick schemes.[4]

Sadly for Manne's idea, Congress moved to regulate this "market for corporate control" with the Williams Act of 1968, before it grew to threaten established businesses. Moreover, prevailing antitrust standards meant that companies that sought to acquire their competitors routinely faced federal scrutiny, yet according to Manne, competitors were those most likely to be able to identify and fix underperformers. Undervalued conglomerates would be safe for years to come—arguably to the detriment of the American economy.

Two changes in 1982 were particularly critical for permitting the reallocation of corporate control: the relaxation of antitrust guidelines and the elimination of state laws limiting "hostile" takeovers. From the perspective of many economists, antitrust rules intended to protect consumers from price-gouging monopolists was actually doing the opposite, by preventing the most efficient businesses from growing as big as they could be.[5] At the Department of Justice, new merger guidelines in 1982 meant that a large market share was no longer a guarantee of prosecution. Horizontal mergers were now possible, but many of the best candidates were locked up inside conglomerates, waiting to be set free by the market for corporate control. The problem was that the laws governing takeovers were made by states, not the Reagan-led federal government, and almost every state had laws making unwanted takeovers very difficult. But in 1982, the Supreme Court ruled in the *Edgar v. MITE* decision that most state laws limiting takeovers were unconstitutional because they limited interstate commerce. In a brief period, the policies protecting undervalued conglomerates (that is, many or most Fortune 500 companies) had been swept away.[6]

Almost immediately, major corporations faced an existential threat that they had never encountered before: the hostile takeover. Outsiders could offer their shareholders a premium to buy enough shares to take control of the company, throw out management, and sell off the parts. These so-called "tender offers" were rare in the 1970s and had almost never affected established companies such as the Fortune 500: There was one in 1980 and two in 1981. But in 1982 there were seven, and between 1984 and 1988, 100 members of the Fortune 500 were subjected to tender offers. There were targets in every industry, from beer (Pabst) and bowling equipment (AMF) to oil (Gulf) and drugs (Richardson-Vicks). From the perspective of executives, it was a corporate apocalypse, equivalent to a plague or an earthquake. One never knew if one's country club buddies would still be employed in the C-suite by the time of the next golf game.[7]

Conglomerates were at the greatest risk, because they were the most systematically undervalued by the stock market. As one law review put it, "The evidence that corporate diversification reduces company value is consistent and collectively damning."[8] Yet diversification was pervasive across corporate America. From the perspective of a corporate raider, 1982 was like wandering into an all-you-can-eat candy buffet.

Over the course of a decade, nearly one-third of the largest industrial corporations had disappeared through hostile takeovers or friendly mergers, resulting in a radical reshuffling of industry boundaries. Those that remained had learned the lesson of focus, and worked hard to jettison any parts that did not fit.[9] By the end of the decade, "focus" had become gospel. Unlike all prior merger waves, the 1980s takeovers left the average corporation smaller rather than bigger, as their unrelated parts were spun off or sold. The size that mattered now was not revenue or employment—neither of those could fend off raiders—but market capitalization, that is, the total value of all the company's shares.

Who does the corporation serve?

HOSTILE TAKEOVERS ON this scale raised an unavoidable question: Who does the corporation serve? Did corporations owe anything to their employees, their customers, or the communities where they operated? Or did corporations exist at the pleasure of their shareholders? When push came to shove, as things often did in takeover battles, the law generally sided with shareholders.

During the postwar era of corporate dominance, there had been a relatively polite consensus on the purpose of the corporation. Indeed, the question of the purpose of the corporation hardly even came up. Corporations existed to serve customers, to provide jobs, to pay taxes. Success was marked by growth in sales and employment; the phrase "shareholder value" was rare outside of business schools. Peter Drucker proclaimed in 1949 that "a growing number of our large enterprises are run on the model which Owen D. Young proposed 20 years ago, when he was head of the General Electric Company: The stockholders are confined to a maximum return equivalent to a risk premium. The remaining profit stays in the enterprise, is paid out in higher wages, or is passed on to the consumer in the form of lower prices."[10] Shareholders were to be seen and not heard.

Economist Carl Kaysen stated that executives in the modern corporation saw shareholders as merely one constituency among many. "No longer the agent of proprietorship seeking to maximize return on investment, management sees itself as responsible to stockholders, employees, customers, the general public, and, perhaps most important, the firm itself as an institution."[11] The "soulful corporation" was a solid citizen, motivated to make its community a better place. This consensus echoed through the end of the 1970s and was reflected in corporate mission statements. Yet by the 1990s, the relevant stakeholders had been winnowed to only one: the shareholders.

The postwar consensus did not disappear completely, in spite of the decade-long dismemberment of the Fortune 500. Some sought to reinstate the old "stakeholder" model through the law. Pennsylvania, for instance, passed an "other constituency" law in early 1990 that aimed to provide a safe harbor for soulful corporations. Pennsylvania had seen a number of takeover battles in which local companies were acquired by out-of-town buyers and later implemented substantial layoffs. The statute, which was bitterly opposed by the institutional investor community and law-and-economics scholars, allowed the boards of Pennsylvania corporations facing unwanted takeover offers to take into account employees and the communities where they operated in deciding whether to allow the company to be sold. Yet most large Pennsylvania corporations opted out of the law because of its potential effect on the company's stock price. By 1990, even those who ran potential targets evidently agreed that shareholders came first.[12]

Shareholders had become increasingly organized and influential, and their voices had perhaps the strongest influence on executive compensation. Influenced in part by economists who wrote rapturously about the benefits of aligning executives and shareholders,[13] boards began to tilt compensation away from guaranteed salaries in favor of stock options and other forms of pay aligned with the company's share price. Within a few years, the majority of a typical top executive's pay came in the form of stock-based compensation. Their day-to-day fiscal well-being was tied quite directly to share price, giving Manne's daily report card some real bite. Once their wallets were captured, executives' hearts and minds were sure to follow.

The "democratization" of the stock market

HOSTILE TAKEOVERS WERE a vivid form of social change, but a quieter revolution was waged in the retirement pension system. Since the end of World War II, pensions were part of the standard employment contract, creating lasting ties between corporations and their workers. Employees had strong financial incentives to spend their careers with a single employer, because those who did so often had a guaranteed income in retirement, as well as other benefits such as health insurance. The Employee Benefit Research Institute reports that, in 1979, 38% of workers were covered by a "defined benefit" retirement plan. By 2011 this had fallen to just 14%; instead, most employee pensions were "defined contribution" (DC) plans that were owned by the employee and invested in the market.[14] The most popular of these plans was the 401(k), named for a section of the tax code that was reformed in 1981 to allow such plans to be used broadly.

The 401(k) was initially intended as a supplement to the traditional corporate pension plan, but within a few years it had become its replacement. Employers preferred DC plans because they were no longer required to maintain a financial commitment to their employees in retirement. Many employees also preferred them because they were portable, allowing workers to move to a new job without threatening their retirement savings.

One result of the move to the 401(k) was that Americans became increasingly invested in the stock market in a direct and visible way. In 1982, only about one in five households had any money invested in the stock market. Buying stocks or mutual funds was largely the domain of the wealthy, and erratic market returns in the 1970s, combined with inflation and the high costs of trading shares, made investing in the market unattractive for the general public. Employees paid little attention to what was going on behind the scenes with the corporate pension; for most, it was simply a benefit to be paid in retirement, not an "investment."

By 2000, however, more than half of all households were invested in the stock market, mostly through mutual funds and retirement accounts (see Figure 5.1). A booming market drew in mom-and-pop investors, and commentators exulted in the new "democratization of the stock market."[15] (Of course, "democratization" did not mean that mom-and-pop shareholders would now be controlling corporate America through some kind of democratic process. That would be socialism.)

Meanwhile, finance became a topic of everyday conversation and pervasive media attention, from the Beardstown Ladies, a group of senior women who formed an investment club, to CNBC. The ups and downs of the market were no longer of interest only to readers of the *Wall Street Journal*—they had become essential parts of peoples' daily information diet. Normal middle-class citizens now identified as "investors," perhaps even more than as "workers." Some checked their

FIGURE 5.1 Percentage of US households owning stock, 1983–2013

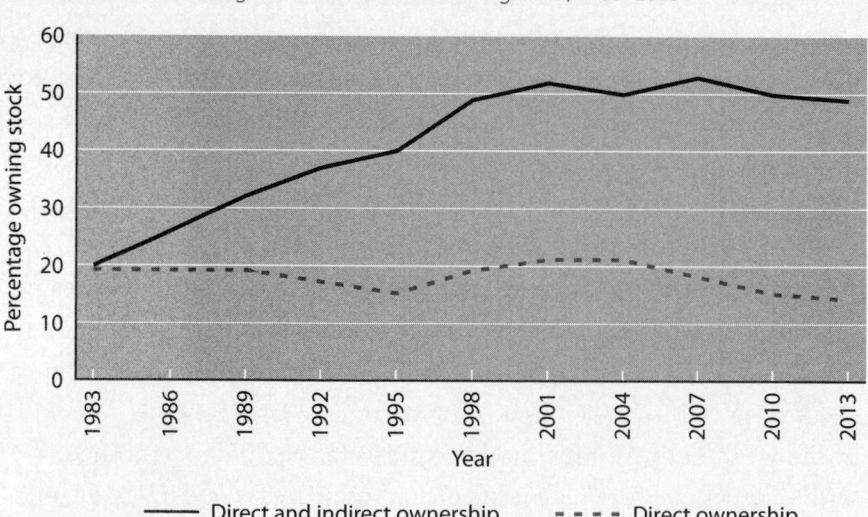

Source: Data from Federal Reserve, *Survey of Consumer Finances*, various years

accounts daily to see how much their portfolio was worth, giving a visceral and emotional connection to the market. If the market was up, one might splurge at a restaurant for lunch; if the market was down, PB&J at the desk.

Widespread interest in financial markets created a popular constituency for market-friendly policies. Conservative commentators in the 1990s saw this as an opportunity, speculating that investors might be more readily persuaded by free-market policies now that they had money at stake. The theory of the investor class argued that stockholders follow different sources of news than nonstockholders, and become more disposed to market-friendly policies. People who check their portfolio every day can see the cash value of public policies for their lives in a way that is much more difficult with, say, regulation of labor organizing or the natural environment. The George W. Bush Administration provided a test case for this idea, pushing policies such as capital gains tax cuts and, more grandly, the privatization of Social Security by essentially creating 401(k) plans for everybody—policies that shareholders seemed to appreciate (at least, much more than nonshareholders). Bush's outreach efforts seemed to work: Research showed households with money that was invested in the stock market (about half the country) came to identify as Republicans to a far greater extent than those not in the market. Surprisingly, these new Republicans largely stuck with the party even after the market collapse of 2008 had left a giant hole in their portfolio. The S&P 500 was 40% lower on the day Bush left office than the day he arrived, giving good reason to question whether Republicans really were the best party for shareholders.[16]

A second result was that the mutual fund industry grew astoundingly large. The 401(k) plans typically offer their participants an opportunity to put their savings into one of a handful of brand-name mutual funds, often managed by Fidelity, Vanguard, or the American Funds. As a result, the shift to DC pensions caused a tsunami of new investment money to be channeled into a handful of mutual fund families. In 1982, the entire industry had about $135 billion in assets under management. Twenty-five years later mutual funds had $12 trillion in assets under management—almost 100 times as much (see Figure 5.2). A few of them each managed over $1 trillion in assets.[17]

The popularity of the stock market created an even more powerful force for shaping corporate governance. Since the Berle and Means book in the early 1930s, it had been universally assumed that corporate ownership was highly dispersed in American corporations. Yet thanks to the flood of new savings into Fidelity, Vanguard, and others, a handful of funds had quietly become the largest owners of corporate America, often owning substantial blocks of 10% or more of a corporation's shares Meanwhile, a new kind of investment vehicle—the exchange traded fund (ETF), which consists of an index of corporate shares that can be bought and sold on the market like an individual stock—was created in the early 1990s, and it quickly became a favorite of retail investors. By 2012, BlackRock, proprietor of the iShares ETF business, had grown to be the single largest shareholder of one in five American corporations, including the three biggest banks (J.P. Morgan Chase, Citigroup, and Bank of America), several of the largest oil companies (ExxonMobil, Chevron, Phillips, and Marathon), as well as AT&T, GE, and Apple.[18] With almost $5 trillion in assets under

FIGURE 5.2 US mutual fund industry assets under management, in billions

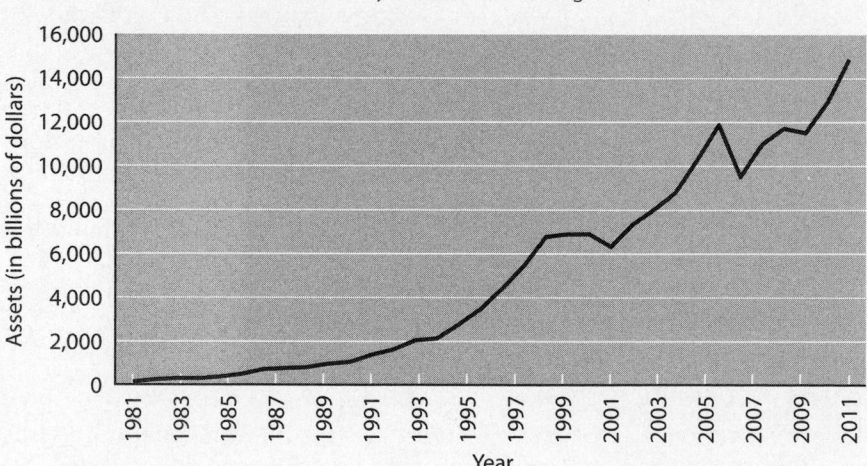

Source: Data from 2014 Investment Company Institute, *Investment Company Fact Book*

management, BlackRock had grown to be far larger than J.P. Morgan was in its heyday a century earlier. Now that financial institutions would live and die by share price and had become the largest and most concentrated owners of corporate America, there was little danger that corporations were going to backslide on their commitment to creating shareholder value.

By the turn of the century, the market's ups and downs were almost inescapable. While fewer people knew how to change their oil or cook a meal, more and more seemed to know what EBITDA (earnings before interest, taxes, depreciation, and amortization) meant, or how to short a stock. College savings and retirement security were heavily invested in the American stock market. The ubiquitous crawl of financial information at the bottom of the TV screen was now of genuine interest to half the population. It was as if we had grown a new organ to sensitize us to how the market was doing.

One stakeholder to rule them all

THE HOSTILE TAKEOVER wave had run its course by 1990, but the focus on creating shareholder value did not. Compensation systems were now heavily tied to share price appreciation, and most of the population was invested in the market by the turn of the new century. Both corporate executives and the broader population had a pecuniary interest in seeing stock prices go up. There was little counterweight in either the political or the economic sphere.

The voice of labor, which might have advocated alternative views of the purpose of the corporation, became muted with the decline of unions. And even the election of a Democratic president in 1992 did not help: No president has ever been more attuned to the vagaries of the financial markets than William Jefferson Clinton, who was informed of the bond markets' reactions to his speeches. And none was surrounded by a more Wall Street-friendly group of advisers, from Goldman Sachs alumni like Treasury Secretary Robert Rubin to Harvard economist Larry Summers. Summers famously quipped that

"Financial markets don't just oil the wheels of economic growth—they ARE the wheels."[19] Of course, the stock market repaid Clinton's devotion in kind, with an almost unprecedented bull market. Thousands of new companies went public, and by 1997 the number of listed corporations in the US increased by 50%. Household investment and market returns created a positive feedback loop right up to the beginning of 2000. The growth did not go on forever, of course, but by now the market had equipped itself with a group of enforcers that focused corporate attention on share price.

Activist shareholders emerged in various guises to make their voices heard. During the takeover wave, a handful of public pension funds joined together to form the Council of Institutional Investors to advocate for best practices in corporate governance. Proxy advisors such as Institutional Shareholder Services emerged to advise funds how to vote at the annual meeting. Research services provided insights into which policies were most likely to create shareholder value. With shares overwhelmingly held by institutions informed by the same set of advisers, the typical company's owners represented a consistent Greek chorus focused on share price.[20] Although they were rarely stirred to overt activism in the 1990s and 2000s, this new group emerged to be more vocal.

Today, even the largest and best-run corporations may be targeted by hedge fund activists. *The Economist* reported in 2015 that 15% of the S&P 500 had been subjected to an activist campaign since the end of 2009, aiming to either change the company's strategy, gain a seat on the board, or fire a manager—usually the CEO. "Since 2011 activists have helped depose the CEOs of Procter & Gamble and Microsoft, and fought for the break up of Motorola, eBay and Yahoo. . . . They have won board seats at PepsiCo, orchestrated a huge round of consolidation across the pharmaceutical industry, and taken on Dow Chemical and DuPont."[21] Even being the most valuable corporation the world has ever known was not sufficient to avoid being coerced: Apple (valued at roughly $700 billion) was targeted because it was evidently hanging on to too much cash for the funds' taste. Given how corporations are owned today—by large index funds advised by proxy advisors who are often sympathetic to the activists' demands—the result is very often that the activists get their way. The only strategy to stay safe is to stay out of the pool, by avoiding a public listing and the demand for ever-increasing shareholder value.

The next chapter describes how the quest for shareholder value has led to the disaggregation of the corporation.

CHAPTER 6

NIKEFICATION AND THE RISE OF THE VIRTUAL CORPORATION

THE TAKEOVER WAVE left the largest American corporations much more focused than they were at the start of the 1980s. One-third of the Fortune 500 had disappeared as independent companies, and those who were left had adopted the gospel of focusing on a core competence. Crossing industry boundaries was now suspect, and "conglomerate" had become an epithet. With the birth of the World Wide Web, corporate focus became even narrower. Companies found it easier and cheaper to outsource whole segments of the supply chain, including manufacturing and distribution. Corporations became increasingly virtual, as the parts of production became like plastic bricks that could be snapped together and broken apart again.

The new model for the corporation was to be like Nike. Nike designs and markets sneakers from its headquarters in Oregon, but hires contractors in East Asia to produce them. Its "core" involves developing intellectual property, not manufacturing physical goods, and it has become one of the most valuable brands in history. Pressed by investors and enabled by the growth of generic suppliers, firms in industry after industry followed a path of Nikefication. Businesses like Sara Lee and Apple jettisoned production to focus on design and brand management. Computers, pet food, pharmaceuticals, shoes, and even government services are increasingly produced by contractors, not the company whose name is on the label.

The Nikefication of American industry has disassembled corporations back into a primordial soup of components. This has had major consequences for employment and corporate accountability. Due to pervasive outsourcing, industries such as computers and electronics have seen a collapse of employment in the United States since the turn of the 21st century. And in a vertically dis-integrated economy, consumers and even companies themselves often have little idea what is going on more than two steps back in their supply chain—whether their products contain "conflict minerals" from the Democratic Republic of Congo, their cocoa was picked by child labor in Ivory Coast, or their garments were sewn under dangerous conditions in Bangladesh. At the same time, activists are demanding greater corporate accountability, leading to a "responsibility paradox."

The birth of the virtual corporation

IN 1993, AT the dawn of the shareholder value age, *Business Week* published a famous cover story by John Byrne titled "The Virtual Corporation." The article stated, "The virtual corporation is a temporary network of independent companies—suppliers, customers, even erstwhile rivals—linked by information technology to share skills, costs, and access to one another's markets. It will have neither central office nor organization chart. It will have no hierarchy, no vertical integration."[1] Where the conglomerates were based on the idea that talented executives could manage everything, the new model suggested that companies should just do one thing really well—design, manufacturing, marketing, whatever—and collaborate with others for the rest.

The virtual corporation was enabled by information technology and the growth of alliances as an alternative to vertical integration. Computer technology allowed designs to be shared and teams to collaborate around the clock. As the kinks were worked out of alliances, they became a low-cost alternative to vertical integration. Some manufacturers who prized their proprietary production processes had begun to loosen their grip on parts of the value chain. Byrne noted how Apple was even willing to trust Sony, a potential competitor, to manufacture its lowest-end laptop computers—at least until Apple had built up its own capacity to produce them itself.

The developments that made the new virtual corporation possible were amplified by the birth of the World Wide Web. *Business Week* shared the vision of Roger Nagel: "He foresees a national information infrastructure linking computers and machine tools across the US. This communications superhighway would permit far-flung units of different companies to quickly locate suppliers, designers, and manufacturers through an information clearinghouse. Once connected, they would sign 'electronic contracts' to speed linkups without legal headaches." What Nagel was describing, of course, was the Web. At the time of the article's publication, the Web barely existed, and there were no commercially available browsers. Companies that wanted to collaborate online used proprietary technology to connect their internal computer systems. This meant that alliances and technology went hand in hand. As Byrne noted, "Until networks and standards let corporations talk to each other across the street or across the ocean, information systems must at least communicate with current and potential partners." Of course, that day was not far off. Thanks to the Web, it is now trivial to create a virtual enterprise, and as we will see, you don't even need to be a corporation to do it.

In some sense, the birth of the virtual corporation was a continuation of the bust-up takeover wave by other means. Bust-up takeovers made clear that the boundaries around corporations were not ever-expanding: Companies could get smaller as well as bigger. Takeovers also highlighted that outsiders might be in a better position to know what should be done inside or outside. Top executives at Beatrice may have believed that the company should make packaged Chinese food, travel trailers, suitcases, and stereos, but the market knew better. Markets love focus. But why should focus stop at industry? It was clear that a company need not manage its own payroll or run its own pension fund or operate its own cafeteria. Maybe it should not be in the business of manufacturing its own products either, or even designing them. What, exactly, was "core"?

Nikefication

PERHAPS NO ORGANIZATION better exemplified the idea of the virtual corporation than Nike. Nike is the largest sneaker and athletic wear company in the world, with annual sales of $28 billion and one of the most recognized brands in history. Yet the 50-year-old firm has only 56,500 employees globally, including part time and retail workers in its 850 stores.[2] Virtually none of them are involved in the actual production of its ubiquitous sneakers. Instead, for decades Nike has focused on design and marketing, while contracting out the rest.[3] Indeed, the earliest years of its existence were spent peddling Japanese sneakers out of the back of a car, only creating its own brand and design in 1971.

Assembling clothes, and even high-tech sneakers, does not require labor with high levels of specialized training. This is why the garment industry is scattered around the globe, and why the clothes at the mall were often made in Bangladesh, Vietnam, Pakistan, Haiti, Honduras, and other low-wage countries. Essentially identical polo shirts or shoes can be produced in any of these countries. Nike was a pioneer in recognizing that their "value added" was in design and marketing, not assembly. Essentially the entire clothing industry follows this model now. Put another way, it is very difficult to find clothes that were actually produced by employees of the company on the label, even at the relatively high end.

The Nike model has been fantastically successful for the company and its shareholders. In the early 1990s, at a time when Apple was still assembling Macintosh computers in its own factories in California, Nike had found a way to focus almost entirely on the cognitive and asset-light work of design and brand management, while contracting out the rest to trusted suppliers in East Asia. Its corporate structure only held on to the high value-added tasks. The attractions of the virtual model were clear. The problem for the model's corporate admirers was that manufacturing jets or cars or computers or pharmaceuticals was not as easily outsourced as making sweatpants and sneakers. Thanks to the Web, that was about to change. Entire sectors, from computers and electronics to drugs to dog food, were about to be Nikefied.

From outsourcing to supply chain management to just doing business

THE NIKE MODEL worked well in clothing because light manufacturing requires minimal equipment, which can be easily transported. At the extreme end, a needle and thread will do the trick, and even electricity is optional. Labor is easily substituted, and it is rare that a supplier is the only one who can provide a unique input. (Exceptions might be Gore-Tex, Polartech, or other branded performance fabrics.) Electronics is different. It requires very specific components, a clean environment, and some level of skill. Electronics can't easily be sent home as piecework, unlike shirts. On the other hand, the equipment and skills that can assemble one kind of electronic product can transfer to assembling another. A Dell PC and a Hewlett-Packard PC are not all that different, and share a lot of parts in common.

This fact enabled the growth of contract assemblers, or what is today known as electronics manufacturing services. EMS companies like Flextronics, Solectron, and Jabil Circuit often started off as "board stuffers," doing the low-skilled work of assembling motherboards for computers, but evolved to take on larger roles. This ultimately included the management of suppliers, final assembly, shipping, and even aftermarket service. By 1998, Ingram Micro was assembling computers for IBM, Compaq, Hewlett-Packard, Apple, and Acer—all on the same assembly line in Memphis. They also installed software and shipped product to final customers in boxes bearing the label of their local dealer.[4]

Didn't this mean that the products were basically interchangeable? Not according to the ironically titled "original equipment manufacturers" (OEMs). A Hewlett-Packard vice president stated that consumers didn't actually care who assembled the product, noting: "We own all of the intellectual property; we farm out all of the direct labor. We don't need to screw the motherboard into the metal box and attach the ribbon cable." Computers had become like sneakers, with brand name and design overshadowing production.

The employment consequences of Nikefication in the American electronics industry have been disastrous. Employment in the industry reached a decade-long high of 1.87 million in January 2001, then rapidly collapsed. Two years later, almost one-half millions jobs in the US had evaporated. By early 2015, another 300,000 jobs were gone.[5] To put this in perspective, Google—perhaps the most successful company of the 21st century—has 53,600 employees globally. The American electronics industry has lost 15 Googles' worth of jobs since the turn of the century. Of course, the fact that these jobs have left the US does not mean that they have disappeared entirely, as electronics assembly still happens in bulk in China. Foxconn alone now employs almost as many people in China as the entire electronics manufacturing industry employs in the US.[6] (But not forever, as Foxconn plans to automate most of its factory work in the coming years.[7])

There was one notable holdout from Nikefication in the computer industry: Dell. Dell Computer originated with Michael Dell's dorm room insight in the early 1980s that the components of a PC were available off the shelf and could be assembled into a product by anyone. Dell's company offered an alternative to IBM that was just about as good, and a lot less expensive. The company also offered mass customization: By doing its own assembly and selling direct to consumers, by phone or over the Web, Dell allowed customers to get precisely what they wanted. While the rest of the industry outsourced production, Dell continued to operate assembly plants in the US, and became the world's largest PC maker. The company's 2006 annual report explained: "Dell believes that its manufacturing processes and supply-chain management techniques provide it a distinct competitive advantage. Its build-to-order manufacturing process is designed to allow Dell to significantly reduce cost while simultaneously providing customers the ability to customize their product purchases." And while others were downsizing, Dell grew from under 35,000 employees in 2002 to over 90,000 in 2007 (albeit mostly outside the US). Yet by

2012, even Dell had given way to Nikefication, noting in its annual report that "third parties manufacture the majority of the client products we sell under the Dell brand. We use contract manufacturers and manufacturing outsourcing relationships to achieve our goals of generating cost efficiencies, delivering products faster, better serving our customers, and building a world-class supply chain."[8] One year later it had gone private to make even more wrenching adjustments. Nikefication had won.

Nikefication was not limited to clothing or computers: Beginning in the 1990s and accelerating after the turn of the 21st century, a number of industries "virtualized" by separating design and brand management from production. By 2007, over 100 brands of pet food sold in North America were produced from the same supplies in the same factory in Ontario. This was revealed when a wave of renal failures among dogs and cats was traced to melamine that had tainted the kibble. The affected brands include Purina, Science Diet, Iams, Del Monte, and several store brands, all produced by Menu Foods.[9]

Pharmaceutical production had also been largely outsourced. A 2014 article notes that "India's pharmaceutical industry supplies 40 percent of over-the-counter and generic prescription drugs consumed in the United States," with its cost advantage stemming in part from the fact that the plants were not subject to routine FDA inspection. China was even further beyond the reach of the FDA, which is a problem given that "the crucial ingredients for nearly all antibiotics, steroids and many other lifesaving drugs are now made exclusively in China."[10] Without inspections, there has been an epidemic of pharmaceutical counterfeiting and safety concerns. In 2008, 81 deaths were linked to tainted heparin produced under contract in China but sold in the US under the Baxter brand name.[11]

For many corporations, Nikefication was not optional. As we saw in the previous chapter, by the 1990s companies faced a Greek chorus of investors and analysts demanding increasing returns, and their executives' fiscal well-being was increasingly tied to the company's share price.

In many cases, the demands of investors were the immediate cause of corporations moving toward the Nike model. Consider

Sara Lee. In 1996, Sara Lee was number 50 on the Fortune 500 list of America's largest corporations. Based in Chicago, Sara Lee was a global company with a large portfolio of well-known consumer brands, including Champion athletic wear, Hanes undergarments, Coach leather goods, Wonderbra, Jimmy Dean sausages, Ball Park Franks, Sara Lee baked goods, Douwe Egberts coffee, and dozens of others. Like many diversified companies, Sara Lee was not getting the stock market valuation it wanted, and so in 1997 the company announced a plan to "de-verticalize" by selling off its factories to outside investors and contracting out production. As its CEO put it, "Slaughtering hogs and running knitting machines are businesses of yesterday." Sara Lee could be more like Nike: light on physical assets and heavy on intellectual property. The more immediate explanation for the shift was that the market did not value tangible assets very highly. The CEO continued: "Wall Street can wipe you out. They are the rule-setters. They do have their fads, but to a large extent there is an evolution in how they judge companies, and they have decided to give premiums to companies that harbor the most profits for the least assets. I can't argue with that." A company can increase its return on assets either by increasing the numerator (raising profits) or decreasing the denominator (shedding assets), preferably using the proceeds to buy back shares—and the latter was often a lot easier.

The company's new mission made clear its priorities: "Sara Lee Corporation's mission is to build leadership brands in consumer packaged goods markets around the world. Our primary purpose is to create long-term stockholder value." Of course, Sara Lee's asset base was not the only thing to shrink in its efforts to please Wall Street. In 2000 the company had 154,000 employees. Twelve years later, after countless spinoffs and a split between the US business (now named Hillshire Brands) and the European business (now Douwe Egbers Master Blenders) it had fewer than 10,000 employees (see Figure 6.1). In 2014, the remaining stub of a company was bought by Tyson Foods, and Sara Lee was gone forever—or at least until a clever MBA bought the brand name to attach to snack cakes made by a generic contract bakery.[12]

FIGURE 6.1 Employment at Sara Lee in thousands, 1995–2012

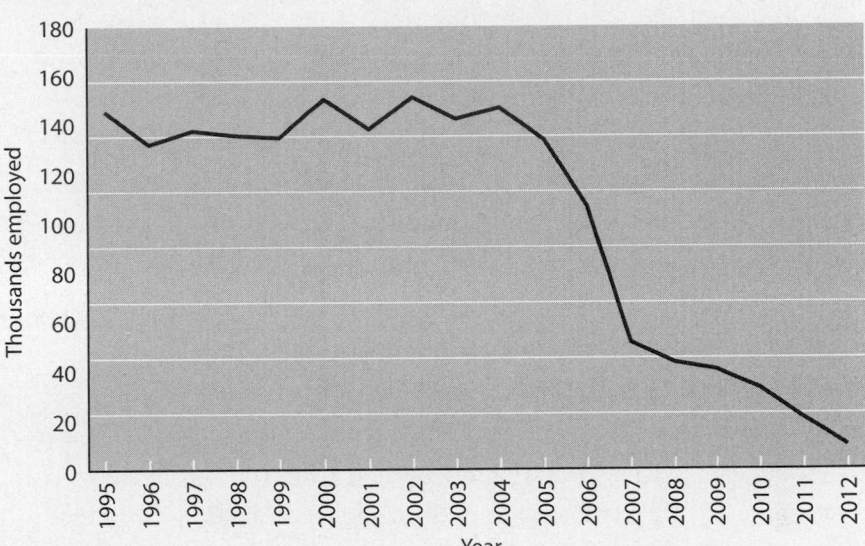

Source: Data from Compustat and company 10-K statements

The responsibility paradox

THANKS TO THE Web and the increasing availability of contractors, and encouraged by the demands of investors, vertical dis-integration has spread to nearly every corner of the American economy. From sneakers to smartphones to pet food to pharmaceuticals to lunch meats, it's a good bet that the products you buy were never touched by employees of the company whose name is on the label. Nikefication is now standard practice across corporate America. While people are generally aware that outsourcing happens, or that Apple does not actually assemble its iPhones, I expect that few realize just how pervasive this practice is. As Edward Snowden's leaks highlighted, even the federal government now relies on outside contractors for protecting diplomats, torturing prisoners, and eavesdropping on the communications of its citizens. (Snowden worked for NSA contractor Booz Allen Hamilton, a century-old management consulting firm that derives almost all its revenues from federal government contracts.) You can't even trust the brand name on a CIA assassination any more.

One consequence of Nikefication is that companies often have little understanding of their own supply chains. When the Rana Plaza factory building in Dhaka, Bangladesh, collapsed in 2013, over 1,100 workers were killed. Investigators found that some of the best-known Western brands were being produced at Rana Plaza and similar dangerous facilities. Yet some of the companies claimed that they were unaware of any untoward conditions in their supply chain, and blamed unauthorized subcontracting for violations. They were many steps removed from the actual manufacture of their branded products, and should not be held responsible for errant contractors.

The Dodd-Frank Act of 2010 included a provision requiring that companies listed on US stock markets (including foreign firms) had to investigate and declare whether any of their products contained "conflict minerals" (tungsten, tantalum, tin, or gold) originating from the Democratic Republic of Congo that might be funding armed conflict in the region. When the first round of reports was due in 2014, roughly four out of five companies reported that they were unable to verify that their products were conflict free.[13] It is easy to see why. For a company like Hewlett-Packard, the minerals that wind up in their computers are four or five steps back in the supply chain, well beyond their line of visibility—particularly after handing assembly and supply chain management off to an electronics manufacturing services firm. Although HP made substantial efforts to gain transparency into the sources of its minerals, some firms may see ignorance as an unspoken benefit of outsourcing. Just as consumers may not know (or want to know) whether their clothes were produced under humane conditions, companies may have little clue how their own branded products are created.[14]

At the same time that companies are outsourcing more and more tasks, the public demands increasing corporate accountability for the actions of their supply chains. Nike was targeted in the 1990s by activists for its use of sweatshops. A 1996 article in *Life* magazine titled "Six Cents an Hour" featured a photo of a Pakistani boy squatting on the floor sewing soccer balls prominently featuring the famous Swoosh logo. Nike's initial response—that it didn't own the factories and therefore was not responsible for their labor conditions—provoked outrage and boycotts, and the company eventually evolved industry-leading standards for suppliers in order to protect their brand image.[15] The same information technology that enables corporations to hire outside contractors around the world also allows journalists and activists to uncover malign conditions in the supply chain, and to demand reform. Much of the world's cocoa supply comes from Ivory Coast, where many farms relied on child labor—in some cases, child slaves and orphans trafficked from neighboring countries such as Mali—to harvest the crop. Boycotts against candy companies were effective in promoting labor standards for most targets (although Hershey, whose voting stock is largely controlled by a trust on behalf of an orphanage in Hershey, Pennsylvania, was one of the last to agree). After Rana Plaza, industry groups adopted standards in the Bangladesh garment industry, although some companies such as Disney simply pulled out of the country entirely.

This is the responsibility paradox: Companies are increasingly dispersed and "virtual," yet we ask them to be responsible for the actions of their suppliers, employees, and even the countries where they do business. After the success of the Nike campaign, activists have made the case that corporations should be held morally and, at times, legally responsible for the actions of their suppliers. Although companies might plead ignorance about what goes on in their value chain, they can no longer easily avoid accountability. In 1996 Unocal was sued by villagers in Burma under the Alien Tort Claims Act for human rights abuses committed by Burmese soldiers guarding the construction of a Unocal gas pipeline. Coca-Cola was boycotted for water depletion and degradation by bottlers in India (most of which are independent companies). Although corporations have gone virtual, the consequences are real, and the public (at least occasionally) expects accountability.[16]

In the next chapter we see how pervasive outsourcing creates another set of dangers for corporations.

CHAPTER 7

THE PUBLIC CORPORATION BECOMES OBSOLETE

THE GROWTH OF generic manufacturers and distributors and the widespread availability of cloud services means that barriers to entry have collapsed in many industries that were previously dominated by traditional corporations. Anyone with a credit card and a Web connection can create an enterprise, from incorporation to production to distribution. The economies of scale that gave birth to the modern corporation have disappeared in many sectors. Lightweight entrants can scale up or down rapidly by renting rather than buying capacity, and their low cost means that in many domains they are a superior choice for consumers. For instance, Vizio (with 200 employees) sold about as many televisions in the United States in late 2007 as Sony (with 150,000 employees).[1] These lightweight firms with modest time horizons have little rationale for bearing the costs of going public. Meanwhile, incumbent firms such as Dell face existential threats requiring substantial and uncertain restructuring, which often results in exiting the stock market.

The decline of the public corporation does not mean that business per se is collapsing. Business will survive in one form or another. There are many ways to organize enterprises, legally and financially, and the current era has seen a flowering of alternative forms. But the public corporation may be like the aristocracy of Western Europe, which still hangs on in some corners but is no longer a dominant force in society.

The pop-up company

SUPPOSE YOU WANTED to start an enterprise without leaving your couch. Is that possible? Imagine a hypothetical product: the iPhone Remote Drone Assassin App. The app would allow users to control weaponized drones for classified operations. The market for the product would include government contractors of various types, as well as freelance operators. The first step is to rent a virtual space at a legitimate-sounding address, preferably in Silicon Valley (to convey high-tech street cred). Next, incorporate online in Liberia, the legal home to many legitimate companies like Miami-based Royal Caribbean Cruise Lines. It's easy and quick, and may have certain unspecified advantages when tax time comes. What about funding? Thanks to the "JOBS (Jumpstart Our Business Startups) Act" of 2012, finding investors online is easy, through various crowdfunding sites. Contract programmers to write the app can be hired via Upwork and several other sites. A manufacturer for the drone itself can almost certainly be secured at Alibaba.com, which includes a vast selection of remote control aircraft vendors in China. Square is a user-friendly payments company that allows anyone with a smartphone or tablet computer to accept credit card payments. Finally, Shipwire will pick up the products from the dock in Long Beach, warehouse them, and distribute them to users. With a few clicks, you can be an entrepreneur.

You might want to go further. Silicon Valley firms almost inevitably have a mythic origin story about the exact coffee house in San Francisco where the idea originated, or the garage in Palo Alto where the prototype was built. It's easiest to hire an online "creative" contractor to generate an appropriate fable. If you want to further burnish your marketability, consider renting a defunct brand name like RCA or Westinghouse for your product, which the older members of the public might vaguely remember and trust.

This scenario is not entirely fanciful. Remember how Michael Dell started a computer company in his dorm room, and ultimately grew it to be the best-selling brand in the US? Today, almost anyone with a credit card and a Web connection can create an enterprise without leaving their dorm room, as the barriers to entry have collapsed in industry after industry. In many sectors it no longer pays to be big and integrated; in others, large-scale generic producers are happy to serve anyone, allowing new competitors to test the waters and rent expanded capacity as needed.

Vizio grew to be the best-selling brand of LCD televisions in the US by 2010, beating Samsung and far outpacing Sony, by offering low-cost TVs assembled by a Taiwanese partner and sold through big-box retailers like Costco.[2] Just as Michael Dell realized that PCs were composed of off-the-shelf components with a superfluous brand name, Vizio's founder recognized that anybody could make a flat-screen TV, and the lowest-cost producer with the best distribution would win. Unlike Dell, however, Vizio chose not to invest in assets or employees: It had fewer than 200 workers when it surpassed Sony, and even today, as it has expanded into sound equipment and laptop computers, it has only 400 employees—about as many as a typical Walmart superstore.

The Flip video camera also grew rapidly from its invention in 2007 to 2009, when it had become a must-have accessory for millennials. With just 100 employees, it had the largest market share in its industry thanks to its clever design and marketing. Cisco bought the company in 2009; two years later, it was closed because Flip was obsolete: Many people who would buy a Flip already had a smartphone that could do much the same thing.[3] Flip was the corporate equivalent of a pop-up restaurant. At four years from birth to market dominance to obso-lescence, Flip was much more efficient than Eastman Kodak, which took well over a century and tens of thousands of career employees to follow this same trajectory.

Compare Vizio and Flip with their better-known competitor, Sony. Sony is one of the most storied brand names in history, known around the globe for products like the Walkman and the Trinitron television. But with 150,000 employees, billions in assets, and expensive real estate in Tokyo, Sony is costly to maintain, and has lost many billions in its electronics business. (It fares much better in life insurance, movies, and music.) A chorus of financial analysts has urged the company to quit the electronics industry entirely. As one analyst put it in 2013, "Electronics is its Achilles' heel, and in our view, it is worth zero. . . . In our view, it needs to exit most electronics markets."[4] Shortly after this report, Sony sold its personal computer business and exiled its television business to a subsidiary. Sony was fitfully exiting the electronics business, just as its analysts asked.

But the music business faces the same form of lightweight competition. Stockholm's X5 Music Group, with just 43 employees, produced 13 of the top 50 selling classical albums in 2010—about the same as Universal, the industry's heavyweight. The company licenses the rights to performances owned by smaller classical music labels and virtually "packages" them into compilations for sale online via iTunes and Amazon. With no need for physical product, the company can be radically tiny yet large in its impact. And unlike Sony and Universal, it does not require corporate jets or skyscrapers.[5] Similarly, whereas Blockbuster had 83,000 employees and 9,000 physical stories at its height, Netflix today has only 2,200 employees and rents server capacity from Amazon.[6] The ability to rent assets and use contract employees allows firms to be tiny and nimble, yet large in impact.

In 1977, sociologists John Meyer and Brian Rowan wrote that "the building blocks for organizations come to be littered around the societal landscape; it takes only a little entrepreneurial energy to assemble them into a structure."[7] At the time they wrote the article, this was poetic and almost whimsical. Today, it is descriptively accurate.

A corporation was once a social institution, with a mission and members and boundaries that separated the inside from the outside. Today it is more like a Web page. What do I mean by this? Right-click on a Web page and choose "View page source." The pleasing coherence of the visual design you saw is replaced by pages of unreadable code. Much of the code is essentially instructions that say: "Go to the database located at the following address and pull an image from here to place in the following location; go to this other database and pull some text from there." It is a series of calls on outside resources that are brought together just in time to convey the image that you see. Vizio,

Flip, and scores of other contemporary enterprises are a lot like this: not an enduring social institution with members and obligations, but a Web page.

The high cost of being a corporation

IT IS USEFUL to recall why we had corporations in the first place. Corporations were created to pursue ventures that required investments that would be too big or too risky to be financed by individuals and families on their own. In the US, the prototypical corporation in the 19th century was the railroad, and later the large manufacturer. These enterprises required funds for tangible capital like land, plant, and equipment. Corporations made sense as a legal form when one needed to own costly and long-lived assets. Thus, the corporation was a good way to finance enterprises characterized by economies of scale, where bigger was cheaper. If the cheapest way to make cars is on a giant assembly line in Detroit employing thousands of people, and to ship them from there to the rest of the country, then it makes sense to form a corporation and issue shares to the public. Many industries looked like this in the 20th century, particularly in the United States, with its enormous continent-wide market connected by railroads and then interstate highways. As business historian Alfred Chandler argued, this is much of the reason that the American economy was "corporatized" at the turn of the 20th century. Large-scale production technologies and the benefits of new methods of management made the modern corporation possible, and perhaps even inevitable given its cost advantages.

There were alternatives in other countries, of course, where giant enterprises were often financed and owned by the national government. In France and even Britain, for instance, many of the best-known large manufacturers and transportation companies were state-owned enterprises. But in the US, giant consumer markets were served by private corporations financed by giant capital markets.

Being a public corporation inevitably brings costs. Raising capital on public markets imposes a set of requirements for accountability and transparency. Investors need some assurance that they will get their money back, and making those assurances believable costs the company money. Some of these costs are explicit. Public companies need to issue quarterly and annual reports explaining what the company does, who is running it, and how it is doing. A public corporation is required to share its balance sheet explaining its assets (what it owns) and liabilities (what it owes). It also needs to issue an income statement documenting its revenues and expenses. A reputable outside accountant to verify these accounts is necessary, and not cheap.

Public corporations are also required to disclose a large number of other things, such as who is on the board and their qualifications and other commitments; how much executives are paid; what risks the company faces; how its labor relations fare; and more. These disclosures are intended to make it easier for investors to assess whether it is sensible to invest in a company, and what it might be worth. They also make it easier for actual or potential competitors to see what the company is up to, which is another kind of cost.

Corporations also face regulations that other forms of business do not. In the US, corporations are created by the states, not the federal government, and states recognize contracts created by other states. This is why Delaware is able to be the most popular state of incorporation by far, even though few companies are actually headquartered there. But the federal government does regulate stock markets and the companies that trade on them. As a result, when Congress wants to shape business behavior, it often does so through regulations of companies listed on American markets. When Congress wanted companies to stop paying bribes in other countries, it passed the Foreign Corrupt Practices Act of 1977, which made it "unlawful for an issuer of securities . . . to make certain payments to foreign officials and other foreign persons." (Notably, the FCPA also applies to the several hundred foreign companies listed on US markets, some of whom grumbled about "regulatory imperialism.") Similarly, the Dodd-Frank Act discussed in Chapter 6 requires US-listed companies to disclose if they are using conflict minerals from the Democratic Republic of Congo in their products.

Corporations that issue shares face a long list of regulations about their corporate governance and other aspects of how they do business, and these inevitably create financial costs. To be clear, I am not arguing against financial regulation, any more than I would argue against going to the dentist or installing smoke alarms, both of which also cost money. Financial fraud at companies like Enron and WorldCom robbed many people of their retirements. Until business is run exclusively by saints, there will inevitably be costs of complying with sensible regulations.

Other costs of being a public corporation are implicit. The public expects things of corporations: safe products, fair wages, decent employee benefits like health insurance, ethical supply chains, social responsibility. When corporations fail to live up to these expectations, their required disclosures are a gold mine of information for journalists and activists who want to hold them to account. Anyone can look up the compensation packages of the top five corporate executives of any listed company for the past 20 years at the US Securities and Exchange Commission's EDGAR (Electronic Data Gathering, Analysis, and Retrieval) website (see Resources). This is why financial publications inevitably fill column space every year with stories about the highest-paid executives, and why it is common to see estimates of the outrageous ratio of CEO pay to that of average workers to document the rapaciousness of corporate America. Now try to find the same information about Koch Industries, which is privately owned and therefore not required to tell the public what it earns.

Social activists also find it much easier to target listed corporations than other kinds of businesses. Fossil fuel companies currently face a global campaign by climate change activists aimed at getting universities, foundations, and other large investors to divest from the sector. Meanwhile, in 2015 ExxonMobil and other oil companies faced a raft of climate-related shareholder proposals: to adopt greenhouse gas reduction targets; to distribute capital to shareholders rather than spend it on capital investments in carbon-intensive projects; to appoint a director with expertise in climate change and renewable energy; to link executive compensation to sustainability performance; and to report on efforts to reduce the adverse effects of fracking.[8] On the other hand, private companies in the fossil fuel business, such as Koch Industries, have no worries about divestment or activist investors.

Finally, beyond the demands of regulators and the scrutiny of media and social movements, public corporations today face unprecedented levels of activism by hedge funds demanding changes in personnel, finances, and strategy. As I noted in Chapter 5, *The Economist* reported in 2015 that 15% of the S&P 500 had been targeted by shareholder activist campaigns since 2009. Their demands typically include some combination of a board seat, a new CEO, a bust-up, and/or a share buy-back. Share price performance is no longer enough to fend off activists: Even Apple, the world's most valuable corporation, was targeted due to its oversize cash hoard. If Apple can't keep its shareholders happy, then no one is immune to shareholder activism.

There have always been costs associated with being a public corporation, but the threshold today is high enough that the costs may not be balanced by the benefits. It is expensive to be Eastman Kodak, or Sony. Both had large and loyal workforces and large obligations to their employees and their communities. Their ability to meet those obligations is what made them stable employers and good citizens. But it also made it hard to adapt to radical changes in cost structures that made Flip and Vizio potent (if ephemeral) competitors. Today, the biggest threats to the security of nation-states often come not from other nation-states but from hackers and paramilitary groups using improvised explosive devices and the Web. Similarly, some of the biggest threats to the viability of the corporation come not from well-capitalized competitors but from low-cost pop-ups.

The low cost of being a project

NIKE DEMONSTRATED THAT the value of sneakers is in the design and the brand, not in the actual physical production or distribution of the shoes. Design and execution can be entirely separated, and consumers do not seem to be bothered by it. The value is in the intellectual property; goods themselves are fungible. As we saw in Chapter 6, this model spread far beyond the garment industry to include computers and electronics, pharmaceuticals, pet food, and almost anything else you can buy in the US. Most consumers are aware that the iPhone, the leading product of our age, is assembled by employees of Foxconn, not by Apple. Aside from occasional concerns about human rights abuses, however, consumers and investors are untroubled by this.

Dell demonstrated that even the design is not always especially important if the price is low enough. Why pay extra for an IBM label when a Dell is just as good, customizable, and a lot less expensive? Vizio took the Dell idea a step further. The designs are thoroughly generic, and there is no customization. But they are much, much less expensive than the name brands like Sony. Unlike Sony, Vizio has none of the baggage (and costs) of being a social institution. And when flat-screen TVs are replaced by implantable 3-D virtual reality brainpods, Vizio will disappear with a minimum of fuss and tears, to be replaced by a new generic implantable brainpod vendor.

There is some irony in the fact that the shareholder-driven outsourcings of the 1990s and 2000s created the infrastructure of generic manufacturing, distribution, business services, and computing power to render the shareholder-owned corporation obsolete. The restructurings of the 1990s were almost inevitably accompanied by a nod to shareholder value, as at Sara Lee. The spread of the virtual corporation model was a boon for generic plug-and-play vendors who could assemble products and manage supply chains, ship goods to consumers, and provide various business services. But once all of these components were available off-the-shelf—not just the physical components, but all the processes needed to do business—it became much easier for anyone to be the next Michael Dell. The economies of scale that made corporations indispensable in the 20th century had now shifted against them.

Surprisingly enough, this often came at the expense of the investor class who had helped make it happen in the first place. If I can use a credit card to start a business that will quickly grow to be dominant, why do I need a venture capitalist? A 2013 article in *The New Yorker* described how the cost of starting up a new venture had collapsed due to the ready availability of plug-in resources.

> Once, an entrepreneur would go to a venture capitalist for an initial five-million-dollar funding round-money that was necessary for hardware costs, software costs, marketing, distribution, customer service, sales, and so on. Now there are online alternatives. "In 2005, the whole thing exploded," [an informant] told me. "Hardware? No, now you just put it on Amazon or Rackspace. Software? It's all open-source. Distribution? It's the App Store, it's Facebook. Customer service? It's Twitter—just respond to your best customers on Twitter and Get Satisfaction. Sales and marketing? It's Google AdWords, AdSense. So the cost to build and launch a product went from five million . . . to one million . . . to five hundred thousand . . . and it's now to fifty thousand."[9]

It is not hard to predict that this cost structure will continue to decline, and it is not just for app startups. Capital equipment has also dropped dramatically in cost, due in large part to CNC (computer numerical control) technology, which acts as the brains of machine tools. A ShopBot router, which could cut plans for much of the furniture in the Ikea catalogue, costs far less than a year of tuition at a private college, and a portable version costs not much more than a laptop. Indeed, outfitting a machine shop is less expensive than sending a kid to college these days. But there is no need to actually purchase or rent the equipment, because membership in TechShop or other similar makerspaces allows makers to use high-end precision equipment for the cost of a gym membership. With easy access to open-source designs, anyone who can assemble Ikea furniture can make it themselves, using their own materials.

What is a "large" corporation?

ONE OF THE most visible consequences in this shift from corporation to project is in the employment practices of the newest companies. For most of the postwar era, the biggest corporations tended to be large in revenues, employment, assets, and market capitalization. Today, these different aspects of "size" are no longer necessarily linked. Walmart is huge in revenues, employment, and market capitalization. General Motors and Kroger are large in revenues and employment but modest in market capitalization (shares value). Facebook is vast in market cap, small in revenues, and tiny in employment.

The five corporations with the largest stock market values and the sizes of their workforces from 1962 to 2012 are shown in Table 7.1. For most of this period, the most valuable corporations were also very large-scale employers, offering relatively secure employment and opportunities to climb a career ladder. By 2012, however, only Walmart among the top five in market value had more than 100,000 employees, and the career ladder it offers to most employees is more

TABLE 7.1 Top five market cap US corporations and the size of their workforces (in thousands), 1962–2012

| 1962 | | 1972 | | 1982 | | 1992 | | 2002 | | 2012 | |
Company	Employees	Company	Employees	Company	Employees	Company	Employees	Company	Employees	Company	Employees
AT&T	564	AT&T	778	AT&T	822	AT&T	313	Exxon	93	Apple	76
DuPont	101	Eastman Kodak	115	Exxon	173	Exxon	95	GE	315	Exxon	77
Exxon	150	Exxon	141	GE	367	GE	231	Microsoft	51	Google	54
GM	605	GM	760	GM	657	Philip Morris	161	Pfizer	98	Microsoft	94
IBM	81	IBM	262	IBM	365	Walmart	434	Walmart	1400	Walmart	2,200

Source: Compustat

of a step stool. Walmart is the largest private employer in the US, Canada, and Mexico. In the US, Walmart has more workers than the dozen largest manufacturers combined. It also has very high turnover, and a large proportion of its workforce is part-time, in sharp contrast to the large-scale employers of the past.

Now consider the best-known companies in the high-tech economy since 2000. How many people do you know who actually work for any of these companies? Unless you live in Palo Alto, the answer is likely to be "none." (If you know someone who claims to work for these companies, odds are good that they are a contractor, not an employee.) As of 2015, Facebook had 1.35 billion users, but only 9,199 employees. Twitter had 288 million monthly users, and 3,638 employees. Dropbox had over 300 million users, and 971 employees—Zynga, 1,974 employees; Zillow, 1,215; LinkedIn, 6,897; Uber, perhaps 2,000; Square, 1,000. Of course, Google—the paradigmatic corporation of the 21st century—is a bit bigger, with 53,600 employees around the world. But the combined global workforces of all of these companies put together is still just 80,000—less than Blockbuster had in 2005, or the number of net new employees GM added in 1942 alone.

We might reasonably ask: Is Facebook a "large corporation"? With a market capitalization close to one-quarter trillion dollars (currently greater than J.P. Morgan Chase, and far more than Citigroup or Bank of America), Facebook seems like a major corporation, and its name is familiar to everyone. Yet hardly anyone actually works there, and in spite of the mythology of the "app economy," hardly anybody makes a living writing apps either (a theme we will take up in a later chapter). And with only $12.5 billion in revenues in 2014, Facebook is only at about the middle of the Fortune 500 (it was number 341 in 2013).

Alternative ways to do business

THE IDEA THAT corporations are somehow in trouble will sound surprising, if not downright ludicrous. We are surrounded by well-known brand names all day, assaulted by advertisements, and marinated in reminders of our corporate society. Our politics is hijacked by "corporate money," and the influence of corporate interests seems to be everywhere. Surely I cannot be claiming that this is all a facade, or that corporations are about to disappear? If anything, it would seem that corporations have never been more powerful.

To be clear, the "corporations" I am describing are those that issue shares on the stock market. It is not the case that all forms of doing business will evaporate, or even that all public corporations are doomed. After all, feudalism is long gone, but we still have royal families in much of Western Europe. What I am claiming is that the public corporation will no longer be the default way of doing business or organizing a postindustrial economy, just as feudalism is no longer the default way of organizing an agricultural economy. The public corporation was well suited to large-scale production and economies of scale. Low entry costs mean that many alternatives become plausible, and if they are cheaper, they will win.

What are these alternatives? Perhaps the most popular is the LLC (limited liability company). LLCs are simple and cheap to set up in almost every state, highly flexible, and easy for tax purposes, as returns flow through directly to owners. It is possible to create an LLC for less than $50 in some states, and for several years now new businesses have been far more likely to organize as an LLC than a corporation. It's a good bet that your local McDonald's franchise or dentist office is organized as an LLC. Even Burning Man, the annual countercultural event in the Nevada desert, is organized by an LLC. LLCs can be quite large too. Companies owned by private equity firms are often organized as LLCs. For instance, after Daimler sold Chrysler to Cerberus Capital Management, it was organized as an LLC. Geoffrey, LLC, is the nominal owner of the Toys"R" Us toy store chain, while its ultimate owners include Bain Capital, LLC.

Legal forms with additional purposes beyond profit are the L3C (low-profit LLC) and the benefit corporation. Alternative ways to channel capital to business include private ownership (for example, family business), private equity, and newer forms such as crowdfunding; these are compatible with alternative legal structures, but LLCs tend to be the default.

Thanks to low barriers to entry, new ways of doing business are proliferating wildly. If creating an enterprise is inexpensive and requires little investment and few dedicated assets, then low-cost legal forms are attractive. And even at a larger scale, the benefits of the public corporation as a legal form are diminishing, due to all the inherent costs mentioned previously.

At the end of the day, the enterprises that survive will be those that provide the goods and services people want at prices they will pay. For most of the 20th century, the efficient size of these enterprises was large, and large corporations often lived a very long time. Today, the efficient size is often very small, and that is likely to mean fewer and shorter-lived corporations. In the next chapter we see how this has led to a long-term decline in the IPO market.

CHAPTER 8

THE LAST GASP OF THE IPO MARKET

THE RANGE OF activities for which the most economical format is to organize as a corporation and sell shares to the public is rapidly diminishing. The parts needed to create an enterprise are often available off the shelf, which allows creating pop-up ventures that are cheaper and nimbler than established corporations. Yet some companies are still doing initial public offerings (IPOs), that is, selling shares to the public in what used to be called a "capital raising." Why?

IPOs offer founders of companies and their financial backers an opportunity to cash in. Going public allows venture capitalists to recoup their investment, lets early employees capture the rewards they were offered, and creates a currency for the company to make acquisitions. There is great appeal in selling shares to the public.

Yet the attraction for buyers is less obvious. Firms that have gone public since the dot-com collapse of 2000 often flout standards of corporate governance (for example, by giving founders permanent control through super-voting shares). Their rationale for going public—to pay off employees and early investors, rather than to raise capital to invest in long-lived assets—suggests that such firms are not sustainable as public companies for the long term, although demand for returns by investors may sustain them for some time.

Three magic words

BY SOME ACCOUNTS, the goal of entrepreneurs everywhere is to sell shares in their business to the public through an initial public offering, or IPO. The IPO offers a chance to pay back early investors and reward employees while also validating the vision of the founders. Going public is a considerable achievement, a major milestone in the life of the entrepreneur and the enterprise. It can also make founders very rich. Not every entrepreneur values going public, however, because of the potential loss of control. Ford Motor Company, an icon of American capitalism, did not go public until 1956, nine years after its founder had died and a half-century after its founding. Henry Ford's mania for control, realized in end-to-end vertical integration, was not compatible with selling shares to the public during his lifetime. Henry allegedly told his son, who advocated going public, "I'll take every factory down brick by brick before I let any of those Jew speculators get stock in the company."[1] (Henry was in the vanguard of industry; not so much when it came to morality.) When the company did eventually go public, the Ford family retained a class of shares that gave it 40% of the voting rights, guaranteeing effective family control in perpetuity.

For much of the 20th century, corporations did an IPO when they had a history of doing business and a plan for profitability in the future. The IPO could raise capital to grow the business, by buying plants and equipment, or stores, or rolling stock. Building giant and efficient factories cost money; so did coast-to-coast distribution networks and department stores. Companies that proposed to go public explained to potential investors how they would use the funds, and why they expected future profits to justify buying their shares.

During the 1990s, however, the IPO became an almost inevitable step in the life of any tech startup, whether or not it had a history of profits, or even revenues. Data from Professor Jay Ritter at the University of Florida show that there were almost 4,500 IPOs from 1990 to 2000.[2] Hundreds of biotech and dot-com companies went public, with limited prospects at best for growing into a real business. It seemed that a great concept—say, selling pet supplies online—was enough to justify an IPO, even in the absence of any revenues or credible plans to make profits. Wall Street firms earned large commissions from IPOs, and early investors looked forward to the one-day pop in price, which some regarded as free money. Going public creates business for a large phalanx of service providers, from lawyers and bankers to accountants and consultants. With the surging stock market of the 1990s, there was plenty of business to go around. IPOs drew in millions of investors around the world, creating a virtuous circle that encouraged entrepreneurship, or at least a lot of vaguely plausible business ideas.

Some months saw scores of IPOs. On November 23, 1999, the following companies were recorded as going public:

- Agency.com (interactive marketing)
- Cartesian, Inc. (consulting to the communications industry)
- Deltathree, Inc. (voice-over-IP telephone services)
- Digital Impact, Inc. (Internet marketing)
- DrugMax, Inc. (distributor of pharmaceuticals and beauty products)
- GetThere, Inc. (web-based travel reservations)
- Official Payments, Inc. (electronic payments for the IRS)
- SmarterKids.com, Inc. (online retailer of children's educational books and games)
- TeleCorp PCS, Inc. (wireless services)
- Teledyne Technologies, Inc. (spinoff of conglomerate Allegheny Teledyne)
- Water Pik Technologies, Inc. (another spinoff of Allegheny Teledyne)

The next day saw three more: Axesstel, Inc. (wireless broadband), KnowledgeMax, Inc. (e-business supply chain management), and PNV, Inc. ("the leading provider of bundled telecommunications, cable television and Internet access services to truck drivers in the privacy and convenience of their truck cabs").[3]

The mania for public offerings was unprecedented. It seemed that almost any vague business concept with a "dot-com" in its name was able to raise millions of dollars from eager investors, many of whom were new to the market. The excesses of the dot-com era are well documented. The rapaciousness of Wall Street and the credulity of investors inflated a bubble that left sophisticated investors dumbfounded. Warren Buffet and other value investors anxiously sat out the frenzy rather than adopting new valuation techniques that were far removed from any reasonable theory of expected profits. The market could not stay this crazy forever.

The high-water mark of this rush of IPOs was March 2000, when the Nasdaq index topped 5,000. Within a few months of reaching this peak, the index had dropped by almost 70%, and it would not pass 5,000 again for almost 15 years. Hundreds of companies disappeared during the burst of the dot-com bubble, and related business scandals emerged, such as the Enron fraud. A series of financial reforms were adopted to limit just how ludicrous firms proposing to raise capital on the public markets would seem, how egregious the misrepresentations of their investment banks, and how extreme the conflicts of interest facing financial analysts. The Sarbanes-Oxley Act of 2002 was the most consequential, creating more rigorous standards for corporate boards of directors, accountants, and financial analysts, and requiring top executives to personally attest to the truthfulness of the company's financial disclosures.

In part as a result of these reforms, the number of IPOs has never returned to the level of the 1990s. Yet they still hold a fascination for outside observers, who see IPOs as a sign of the ruddy health of American business. To this day, entrepreneurial business plans almost inevitably include an "exit strategy" that entails dumping shares on an unwary public.

IPOs in the 21st century

THE NUMBER OF IPOs dropped dramatically after 2000, and they have never recovered their old allure (see Figure 8.1). In the 14 years since 2000, there have been roughly 1,600 IPOs in the United States. Many of these were not new businesses, but companies that had gone

FIGURE 8.1   US initial public offerings (IPOs) by year, 1980–2014

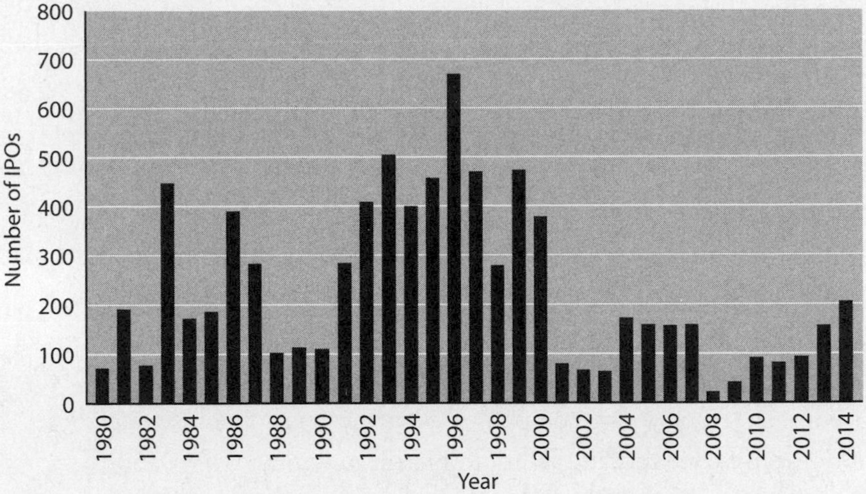

Source: Data from Professor Jay Ritter, University of Florida, http://site.warrington.ufl.edu/ritter/ipo-data/

bankrupt (Northwest Airlines, General Motors), been taken private (Dominos Pizza, Celanese), or were being spun off.

Commentators have offered many reasons for the IPO drought, with "overregulation" being one of the most prominent. Marc Andreessen, a founder of Netscape—whose 1995 market debut was the starting gun for the dot-com race—stated that after 2000:

> A whole set of "closing the barn door after the horse had run out" kind of things happened. Sarbanes-Oxley happened. The irony of Sarbanes-Oxley was that it was intended to prevent more Enrons and WorldComs but it ended up being a gigantic tax on small companies. . . . The compliance and reporting requirements are extremely burdensome for a small company. It requires fleets of lawyers and accountants who come in and do years of work. It's this idea that if you control everything down to the nth detail, nothing will go wrong. It's this bizarre, bureaucratic, top-down mentality that if only we could make

everything predictable, then everything would be magic, everything would be wonderful. It has the opposite effect. It's biased
enormously toward companies that are big enough to hire fleets
of lawyers and accountants, biased against companies that are
very young and for whom there's still a lot of variability.[4]

Andreessen, now a venture capitalist, also notes that the compo-
sition of the market has shifted from individual investors and mutual
funds to hedge funds, short sellers, and other short-term traders who
are highly attuned to moment-by-moment price fluctuations. This can
make the market more volatile and thus more hazardous for newer
ventures. "[F]or young companies, everything is connected: stock
price, employee morale, ability to recruit new employees, ability to
retain employees, ability to sign customer contracts, ability to raise
debt financing, ability to deal with regulators. Every single part of your
business ends up being connected and it ends up being tied back to
your stock price"—which can be whipsawed by short-term investors.
He concludes: "The result of all that is the effective death of the
IPO"—that is, for at least small-cap firms.

Although blaming regulation for economic woes is a reflexive
response for some, one reason for the shortage of IPOs that has
received less attention is that companies simply don't need the money.
We saw in Chapter 7 that it had become much, much cheaper to
launch a company these days. It is not surprising that venture capitalists want to blame regulation, because the alternative is an existential
threat to their industry. One venture capitalist noted the implications
of this new system of low-cost startups:

> "The model that has existed for the past fifty years, with
> people such as ourselves being the gatekeepers of money
> between big institutions and entrepreneurs, is going to at
> least decline as a percentage of the dollars that get invested in
> startups," he said. Instead of raising investment cash, V.C. firms
> could start investing their own capital; the rest would come

from crowd-funding. They'd be traffic directors instead of gate-keepers. . . . What we're seeing now is literally a shift in the way that people do business—a shift from hierarchical architectures to networked architectures.[5]

If regulations make going public costly, short-term traders make it risky, and the low cost of entry makes it unnecessary, then why do companies still do IPOs? This is not an idle question. A company's IPO prospectus includes a required section titled "Use of proceeds." Consider what Facebook has said about how it would use your investment dollars:

> The principal purposes of our initial public offering are to create a public market for our Class A common stock and thereby enable future access to the public equity markets by us and our employees, obtain additional capital, and facilitate an orderly distribution of shares for the selling stockholders. *We intend to use the net proceeds to us from our initial public offering for working capital and other general corporate purposes; however, we do not currently have any specific uses of the net proceeds planned.* . . .
>
> *. . . Pending other uses, we intend to invest the proceeds to us in investment-grade, interest-bearing securities such as money market funds, certificates of deposit, or direct or guaranteed obligations of the U.S. government, or hold as cash.* We cannot predict whether the proceeds invested will yield a favorable return. Our management will have broad discretion in the application of the net proceeds we receive from our initial public offering, and investors will be relying on the judgment of our management regarding the application of the net proceeds.[6] [emphasis added]

In other words: We are selling shares to create a market to sell our shares. We have no use for the funds we are raising, and will put them in the bank until we have a good idea. Trust us. Also, we might make some acquisitions.

This is not unique to Facebook. Of course, there are good reasons for companies to want to be vague about how they will use your money, but there are also very good reasons for buyers of their shares to demand more information about where their money is going.

The two most obvious reasons that companies want to go public are to pay off their early investors, and to give employees who have been compensated with shares a chance to cash in. While this may be a good reason for the company to want to sell its shares, it is hardly a good reason to buy. There are entire categories of bad investments premised on the idea that later investors pay off the early investors (for example, Bernie Madoff).

A third reason to go public is to be able to use the company's shares to make acquisitions. Facebook famously bought WhatsApp, a phone app for sending instant messages, for $19 billion, even though some found WhatsApp to be largely indistinguishable from a half-dozen other instant message apps. An acquisition like this would have been much harder without going public. As Google, Facebook, and Amazon expand into varied unrelated industries (virtual reality goggles, self-driving cars, smartphones), often via acquisitions, they seem to be following the same course as the conglomerates of the 1960s, becoming mutual funds with high overhead.

A fourth rationale for going public is that the proceeds will be used to hire really smart people who will come up with highly profitable ideas in the future. This is comparable to the mission of one company founded during the South Sea Bubble of 1720: "a company for carrying on an undertaking of great advantage, but nobody to know what it is."

It is easy to see why companies might want to go public, in a world full of investment capital seeking an outlet. It is much harder to conceive why investors would hand their money over to such companies.

IPOs and the death of corporate governance

THE DROUGHT OF IPOs since 2000 is often blamed on regulations intended to rein in reckless corporate behavior by enhancing "corporate governance." Corporate governance refers to all the things that shape how corporations make decisions and are held accountable, such as who is on the board of directors and how it is structured; how shareholders influence corporate decisions through annual elections or activism; the actions of accountants, bankers, financial analysts, and other gatekeepers; the stock market itself and how it prices shares; and the "market for corporate control" that allows outsiders to take over a company whose internal management has failed.[7]

There are certain widely shared standards of what good corporate governance entails. "Good" in this case usually means "good at ensuring that the company does what's best for the long-term interests of the company and its shareholders." Some basics include having a well-qualified board of directors composed primarily of outside directors who are independent of management; incorporating in a state with high legal standards; using a reputable accounting firm to audit the company's books; and avoiding measures that protect the company from outside oversight (such as takeover defenses). A bedrock principle is that control of public corporations should be "contestable," that is, that the decisions of management and the board of directors are not insulated from outside oversight (for example, by activist shareholders or potential takeovers).

Yet IPO firms in recent years have often violated one of the most basic principles of corporate governance: that each share should be entitled to one vote, so that voting rights correspond to how much a shareholder has invested in the company. "Unequal voting rights" or "dual class capitalization" has a long history, and many household names have classes of stock that give founders or their families voting rights that ensure their control. For instance, Phillip Knight controls a substantial amount of Nike's voting stock and has the rights to appoint board members.

This kind of structure is most common in the newspaper business. The *New York Times*, the *Wall Street Journal*, *News Corporation*, and many others guaranteed their founders effective control through supervoting classes of stock. The rationale was noble: For the press to serve its essential functions in a democracy, it cannot be subject to undue commercial pressures. If the *New York Times* is not earning enough profits, or alienates a major advertiser through its reporting, activist hedge funds cannot pressure it to sell out its principles merely for cash. Research suggests that structures like this can lower shareholder returns, but investors know that going in. If you are going to invest in a newspaper, you have to accept the risk that it will not always do what is most profitable.

When Google went public in 2004, it gave its founders 10 votes per share, while the public got only one vote per share. As Google's IPO prospectus pointed out:

> Larry, Sergey, and Eric will therefore have significant influence over management and affairs and over all matters requiring stockholder approval, including the election of directors and significant corporate transactions, such as a merger or other sale of our company or its assets, for the foreseeable future. In addition, because of this dual class structure, our founders, directors, executives and employees will continue to be able to control all matters submitted to our stockholders for approval even if they come to own less than 50% of the outstanding shares of our common stock. This concentrated control will limit your ability to influence corporate matters and, as a result, we may take actions that our stockholders do not view as beneficial. As a result, the market price of our Class A common stock could be adversely affected.[8]

In short, if Google's founders decided to sell the company to the government of China, with Tibet thrown in as a sweetener, they could do so. Outside shareholders were willing to take this deal, and thus far they have not been too disappointed. (Although in 2014 there was a shareholder proposal seeking to switch to one-share, one-vote, with a predictable outcome.) Certainly, Google might reasonably invoke the precedent of the *New York Times*: What if hedge funds wanted Google to be evil, in spite of its motto?

But since the 2008 market crash, an unprecedented number of IPO companies have given their founders and other insiders voting rights that guarantee their control in perpetuity—a feature that typically lowers shareholder returns. One study found that more than 10% of IPO companies from January 2010 to March 2012 had dual-class voting structures that gave their founders super-voting rights (which has come to be called the "Zuckerberg grip"). These include LinkedIn (10 votes per share), Zillow (10 votes per share), Yelp (10 votes per share), Zynga (a B class with 7 votes per share and a C class with 70 votes per share), and Groupon (which awarded its founders an astounding 150 votes per share).[9] In other words, far from being bullied by their shareholders, the founders of these firms have found a way, in effect, to maintain uncontestable and eternal control. And while Google might have a plausible First Amendment case, it's hard to see how an online coupon vendor or videogame producer can justify such structures.

Once again, Facebook stands out for its distinctive governance structure. Its Class B shares enjoyed 10 votes per share. They were two-thirds owned by Mark Zuckerberg, giving one person over 50% of the company's total voting power. From the prospectus:

> Because we qualify as a "controlled company" under the corporate governance rules for publicly listed companies, we are not required to have a majority of our board of directors be independent, nor are we required to have a compensation committee or an independent nominating function. In light of our status as a controlled company, our board of directors has determined not to have an independent nominating function and has chosen to have the full board of directors be directly responsible for nominating members of our board, and in the future we could elect not to have a majority of our board of directors be independent or not to have a compensation committee.[10]

When Facebook went public in 2012, it erected a fortress against outside shareholders and gave dictatorial powers to one 28-year-old. It is perhaps not surprising that its share price dropped by half on its first day of trading. What is more surprising is that it not only recovered, but showed impressive returns. With revenues of only $12.5 billion in 2014, it is nonetheless able to make multibillion dollar acquisitions on the whim of its CEO.

Fifteen years after the dot-com bubble burst, and along with it all of the reforms in corporate governance that followed, the most high-visibility entrepreneurial companies of the high-tech economy have abandoned basic shareholder protections. It is possible that Google, Facebook, Zynga, Groupon, and the rest are intended as benevolent dictatorships, with their visionary founders protecting the vital missions of their enterprise from the depredations of short-term shareholders. Perhaps Mark Zuckerberg is the Web's Lee Kuan Yew. But a betting man might think of this as a great opportunity to short in anticipation of the next bubble burst.

The disappointing job creation of IPO firms since 2000

ONE OF THE great fears about the decline in the IPO market is that potential high-growth companies would not be able to raise capital to build facilities and hire people. No IPOs, no jobs. The JOBS Act of 2012 was premised on the idea that access to the public markets was key for job-creating new ventures. Companies with less than $1 billion in revenues would be defined as "emerging growth companies" and exempted from some of the requirements of the Sarbanes-Oxley Act, and would make it easier for companies to raise capital through crowdfunding (for example, by using websites). As we have seen, there is reason to be skeptical about whether access to capital was the reason the economy was not creating many jobs in new companies. Some of the "biggest" tech companies, with multibillion dollar valuations, have surprisingly few actual employees.

So do companies create jobs after they go public? To address this question, I assembled annual employment data for every company that went public in the US beginning in 2001 using the Wharton Research Data Services. It is, unfortunately, not as easy to answer the question about job creation as you might guess. One approach is to measure direct employment. American public corporations are required to report the size of their global workforce every year on the Securities and Exchange Commission's Form 10-K. I examined these figures for every company from the first year they reported after their IPO to the last year they were in the dataset (usually 2014), taking the difference to represent job creation.[11]

Of the roughly 1,600 companies in this group over 14 years, the median IPO firm grew its employment by 51 jobs. One thing that stands out is how many companies actually *shrank* after going public. KBR, an engineering company spun off from Halliburton, reported 56,000 employees in 2006 (its IPO year) and only 25,000 in 2014, shrinking by 31,000. Ally Financial (formerly GMAC) had 28,000 employees in 2000 but only 7,000 in 2014, after its bankruptcy and IPO. Armstrong World Industries shrank from 14,500 to 7,400 after its IPO; BearingPoint shrank from 10,000 to 2,500; and so on.

At the other extreme, there were a handful of companies that saw substantial growth in their job rolls, but on closer inspection this growth often turned out to represent acquisitions rather than organic job creation. Moreover, many of the jobs created were part-time, seasonal, and low-wage. Those companies that ranked in the highest job growth (with number 1 as the highest below) include:

1. Brookdale Senior Living, which went public in 2005, grew from 16,000 to 82,000 jobs in 2014 (52,500 full-time, 29,500 part-time), but this was almost entirely through roll-up acquisitions in the fragmented senior care industry.

2. Synnex, leaping from 1,664 to 64,000 jobs. But the vast majority of those jobs came from its 2013 acquisition of IBM's global business process outsourcing unit. This was job shuffling rather than growth.

3. GameStop, a strip-mall videogame retailer that operates 6,700 stores around the world and employs at each "on average, one manager, one assistant manager and between two and ten sales associates, many of whom are part-time employees. . . . We have approximately 18,000 full-time salaried and hourly employees and between 29,000 and 55,000 part-time hourly employees worldwide, depending on the time of year."

4. Google, which grew from 3,000 at its IPO in 2004 to 53,000 in 2014, through a mix of organic growth and acquisitions.

5. Chipotle Mexican Grill, which grew from 13,000 in 2006 to 53,000, "including about 4,590 salaried employees and about 48,500 hourly employees."

6. CBRE Group, a commercial real estate holding company, which expanded from 13,500 to 52,000—again, through roll-up acquisitions in a fragmented industry.

7. Texas Roadhouse, a restaurant chain, which grew from 9,700 to 43,300, of which many are part-time.

The number of full-time US jobs created by the top 10 IPO companies this century has been quite modest. For comparison purposes, GM added 150,000 people to its payroll in 1942 and 1943, and the US economy created 257,000 jobs in January 2015 alone. Wherever these jobs are coming from, it is not driven by IPOs. With the notable exception of Google, the jobs that are created by IPO companies are often part-time and in low-wage occupations in food service and retail. Google's job growth, averaging 5,000 per year since its IPO, is a bright spot, but it is almost utterly unique in the tech sector.

There is some evidence that the JOBS Act has increased the number of IPOs slightly—one study estimates that 21 more firms per year went public after the Act than would have been expected. Many of these are biotech companies (SIC code 2836), which benefit from the reduced disclosure requirements under the JOBS Act. But the median biotech firms that went public after 2000 had only 49 employees in 2013, and all 100 of these companies put together had fewer than 8,000 employees.[12] (Notably, over 90% had no profits.)

Biotech IPOs will not create a surge in employment, revenues, or profits in the foreseeable future.

IPOs may also be bad for innovation: According to a study by Shai Bernstein at Stanford, companies that become IPOs subsequently see a decline in the quality of their patents, a loss of innovative employees, and a decline in the productivity of remaining employees, relative to firms that filed for an IPO but then withdrew.[13]

It seems that the stock market is largely irrelevant for creating new jobs in the US, and making it easier to go public is unlikely to change things. IPOs no longer provide much information about the health of the real economy, particularly the part involving employment.

IPOcalypse now?

POLICYMAKERS AND PUNDITS have placed a great deal of faith in the power of entrepreneurship to create new job-generating enterprises. Their creed is that unleashing entrepreneurs and providing them with financial capital will give them the incentives and the ability to build enterprises to take the place of the Eastman Kodaks and Westinghouses of old. But this faith-based economic policy is rooted in an outdated view of how the economy works. Entrepreneurs today, guided by their investors, avoid buying equipment or hiring employees that might tie them down. Going public is unnecessary and perhaps even dangerous; those who do it often go out well armed with defenses against their shareholders. Many firms that go public don't need the capital they are raising, or they use it to make acquisitions, not to build capacity. In this way they mirror established companies, which today use much or most of their profit to buy back their own stock rather than investing in new factories or stores.

At the time of this writing, IPOs have experienced a modest resurgence. But given that the large majority of companies going public have no profits and create little employment, it is unclear how this will drive the economy forward. Moreover, the governance practices of the most visible technology firms suggest that eventually the market will turn against them.

CONSEQUENCES OF CORPORATE COLLAPSE

PART III

CONSEQUENCES OF CORPORATE COLLAPSE

POSTWAR AMERICAN CORPORATIONS created a social welfare system in which employers, rather than governments, provided health insurance and retirement security. Beginning in the early 1980s with the 401(k) plan, which replaced the traditional defined benefit pension, many corporate employers have abandoned these responsibilities, and the largest employers today (nearly all of which are in retail) provide minimal benefits. Moreover, the loss of public corporations means fewer domestic investment options for those saving for retirement. Retirees in coming decades face a highly uncertain future due to the retrenchment of the corporation.

The growth of large corporate employers in the postwar period corresponded to a substantial drop in inequality in the US. Corporations equalized compensation systems across the economy and provided career ladders that enabled individuals to move into the middle class. Nikefication and the replacement of manufacturing with retail has led to a polarization of labor markets. As employment has become dispersed, inequality has grown.

As inequality has increased, opportunities to move up in the world have become more limited. In the postwar era, the path to individual prosperity was straightforward: (1) study hard and attend the most prestigious college you can; (2) major in something practical, like engineering or computer science; (3) get a job with a name-brand corporation in an industry with good growth prospects; (4) if your employer does not have a generous pension plan, put your retirement savings into a diversified mutual fund; (5) retire to a Boca Raton condominium in comfort. Without stable corporate employers, however, this system breaks down, and the pathways to upward mobility are inscrutable. We now live in a Powerball lottery economy in which a handful of individuals strike it rich for reasons that are effectively random—say, buying and selling a house in Florida at just the right time, or writing a good-enough app in the early months of the iPhone that becomes a best seller—while most of us plod along and hope for the best.

Nostalgia for the disappearing public corporation may be a bit misplaced. For over a century, "corporate" has been an epithet, and Progressives and others have lamented the concentration of economic power that the public corporation brings. More recent critics have described how a monomaniacal focus on shareholder value has made our economy more prone to boom-and-bust cycles. Prospective benefits of the declining corporation include a potentially reduced influence of Wall Street; greater economic diversity as new forms are developed; new forms of entrepreneurship not premised on the narrow path to IPO; and open space for alternative economic formats that might be more locally attuned and innovative (for example, cooperatives). In place of the 20th-century "redwood forest economy," perhaps we will see something more like a tropical rainforest emerge through a diversity of local initiatives.

CHAPTER 9

THE DISAPPEARING SOCIAL SAFETY NET

AFTER THE END of World War II, American corporations and their workers forged a compact that provided a safety net for employees and their families. The standard employment deal at a major corporation included health insurance for employees and their dependents and a guaranteed pension payout at retirement. The system was geared toward companies that expected to last indefinitely, and employees who expected to stay there for their entire careers. While this might have made sense in the decades immediately following World War II, when big American companies saw an endless horizon of growth, the strains in the system began to appear in the 1980s. It was costly for companies to hold up their end of the bargain, and not all employees wanted to stay at the same job forever.

Beginning in the early 1980s, many corporate employers began to abandon their traditional benefits. Big companies shifted to "defined contribution" pension plans and streamlined their health benefits, particularly for retirees. As a result, most workers nearing retirement today have far too little savings and will end up relying almost entirely on Social Security and Medicare. Meanwhile, the largest employers today (nearly all of which are in retail) provide minimal benefits, while many new companies aim to keep their employment rolls as small as possible, relying instead on temporary and contract workers who do not receive benefits.

America created a corporate-centered system of social welfare provision in the postwar era that was unlike any other advanced economy. As the traditional corporation retrenches, we are witnessing the collapse of that system.

Someone to watch over me

EVERY SOCIETY CONFRONTS the question of who should take care of us when we are sick, or when we cannot work, or when we get old. In agricultural societies it might be the extended family or the village. Mediaeval feudalism established mutual obligations between lords and their dependents. Urbanized industrial societies severed these traditional bonds, and social welfare often fell to solutions such as voluntary mutual aid organizations (e.g., Britain's "friendly societies"). Of course, when medical care was more low tech and people didn't live much past working age, the demands for social welfare did not need to be so costly. But as medical care improved and became more expensive, and life expectancies increased, the cost of social welfare provision also grew.

After the end of World War II, many European nations expanded their welfare state to provide access to health care and income security as a right for all citizens. Britain's Beveridge Report, formally known as the report on "Social Insurance and Allied Services" and written at the height of World War II, laid out a widely influential blueprint for the welfare state that was to emerge after the war.[1] The report stated that society faced five giant evils—"Want, Disease, Ignorance, Squalor, and Idleness"—and laid out a vision for postwar reconstruction to address these evils. The new welfare state included a National Health Service to provide medical treatment for all (established in 1948) and the expansion of the National Insurance scheme to provide social security "from the cradle to the grave." After the devastation of the war, and in spite of the state of the economy, the new system was enormously popular. It was widely considered to be the right thing to do. Across Europe, similar plans spread in the years after the war, and while the specifics differed by country, there was broad agreement that these functions were most effectively organized by governments.

The United States, on the other hand, went in a completely different direction. Social welfare services were to be provided by employers—mostly corporations—and not by governments. The idea of benevolent employers providing social services to their employees was not new. Company towns like Pullman, Illinois, which made railroad cars in the second half of the 19th century, offered a full set of amenities for employee-residents, and many union-averse employers like Eastman Kodak provided extensive employee benefits even during the Depression.[2] During the war, employers who were unable to raise wages due to legal restrictions sought to lure workers with nonwage benefits such as health care.

Thus, while Western Europe saw postwar reconstruction as a time to establish a new social contract between citizens and government, the US resisted the expansion of government services, and even the labor unions who had advocated the expansion of Social Security backed off in the face of strong political resistance.

The signal event of the new system was the Treaty of Detroit, a labor agreement between General Motors and the United Auto Workers signed in 1950 (see Chapter 4). The agreement extended the kinds of benefits normally restricted to managers to the broader blue collar workforce: a pension plan, health insurance coverage that ultimately extended into retirement, and cost-of-living adjustments for wages. Later agreements included supplemental unemployment benefits for laid-off workers. Dependents were covered by health insurance as well. Through pattern bargaining, the Treaty of Detroit spread quickly to the other automakers, and then to steel producers, and then to "major employers" more broadly. Within a few years, corporate employers were, in effect, the American version of the welfare state.[3]

From a contemporary perspective, this system seems odd, if not downright insane. Jobs come and go, companies come and go, people move around. Why in the world should access to health care or retirement income be tied to the breadwinner's current employer? Walmart, America's largest employer by far, has annual turnover of more than 50%, and upwards of half the population changes jobs every year. How could it make sense to change health care and pension plans as often as someone changes jobs? The whole thing only seems reasonable if we imagine that the typical job is with a large-scale, long-lasting employer that could shoulder the expense of running such plans.

Why should corporations provide benefits?

FROM AN ECONOMIC perspective, we might ask why employers provide any benefits at all. Why not just pay cash and let workers decide whether to spend it on health insurance and retirement savings, or on a bigger house or a vacation to Jamaica? If pensions and health insurance became part of the standard employment package across corporate America, there must have been a good economic rationale—otherwise, clever employers would have skipped the benefits and out-competed their more benevolent rivals.

One explanation is that sometimes companies and employees both benefit from staying together for a long time. When employees learn skills that are especially useful to a particular employer, and not as valuable elsewhere ("firm-specific human assets" in the jargon), it makes sense to protect their relationship.[4] Promising a pension that gets more generous over time encourages workers to stay for their whole career, and to avoid doing things that will shorten that career. But if specialized skills explain why companies provide benefits, then why don't they offer wildly different packages to different employees, depending on how specialized they are? And why would automakers like GM offer such expansive benefits to their production employees? After all, they had spent decades refining their assembly lines so that any given job was as unskilled and easily replaceable as possible. What economic purpose was served by offering pensions and health insurance for retirees?

Perhaps the most straightforward answer is that it was an accident of history. In 1949 GM had enjoyed the most profitable year that any American corporation had ever seen. It was arguably the world's largest and most successful manufacturer, facing a powerful and restive union. It could afford to be generous; it could not afford another strike like the one in 1945–46. Professor J. Adam Cobb of the Wharton School found that the negotiation of the Treaty of Detroit was one of the most fraught incidents in American labor history in which some of the tectonic plates of economics, politics, and personality collided to yield a document that was the Magna Carta of the postwar employment relationship. The employment practices of GM set an example for the rest of industry.

Moreover, once these policies were in place, they expanded the possibilities for future bargains. In any given wage negotiation, it might make more sense to trade off future benefits (say, a more generous pension plan, or more extensive health insurance for future retirees) for current wages. Such benefits will be paid on someone else's watch, so why not be generous?

When the bills come due

EXPENSES CAN'T BE deferred forever, and by the early 2000s the costs of being a benevolent employer were becoming clear to both major corporations and municipal governments across America. In March 2006, GM's CEO Rick Wagoner stated, "Our legacy costs in pensions and health care are an area of significant competitive disadvantage for us. . . . We're now subject to global competition. We're running against people who do not have these costs, because they are funded by the government."[5] The CEO of the company that had almost single-handedly created the American corporate welfare system was now ruing how that system had placed them at a competitive disadvantage. It was, put bluntly, a lot cheaper to operate in a country with a strong welfare state. Socialism turned out to be good for business.

The amounts involved were not trivial. GM's costs for retiree health care were estimated to have risen from a few hundred dollars per year for each retiree in the early 1990s to $15,000 in 2007, with more cost increases looming into the indefinite future. Thus, in July 2008 GM wrote to its salaried retirees and their surviving spouses:

> Since the first of this year, US market and economic conditions have become significantly more difficult. These conditions, along with the rapid change in automotive industry sales mix, require us to take further actions that will position GM for sustainable profitability and growth. As a result, GM is announcing a change to the GM Salaried Health Care Program. Effective January 1, 2009, GM is canceling health care coverage for salaried retirees and their dependents age 65 or older. Instead, eligible salaried retirees and surviving spouses over age 65 will receive a monthly pension increase of $300. This pension increase is designed to help offset some of your health care costs in retirement.[6]

By June 1, 2009, GM had filed for bankruptcy. (It would be followed into bankruptcy by the City of Detroit, which had its own pension woes, in July 2013.)

By following its own exceptionalist path, the US had ended up with a system of employer-based health care financing that managed to be far more expensive, with far spottier coverage, than any other advanced economy.

The advent of Obamacare may be the final nail in the coffin of employer-provided healthcare. Scores of well-known companies quickly moved to shift their retirees to health exchanges after the passage of the Affordable Care Act, and Neil Irwin of the *New York Times* wrote that "by 2020, about 90 percent of American workers who now receive health insurance through their employers will be shifted to government exchanges created by the health law, according to a projection by S&P Capital IQ, a research firm serving the financial industry."[7]

The corporate pension system, on the other hand, was at the end of an extended transition that had begun in the early 1980s. The traditional corporate pension was a "defined benefit" (DB) plan. Companies promised a monthly payout in retirement based on a worker's years of service and set aside funds that were invested with such payouts in mind, typically by an outside fund manager. Nearly 40% of all private-sector employees were covered by such plans in 1979, according to the Employee Benefit Research Institute. It was a central element of the standard employment package. Another kind of pension, more common among executives, was the "defined contribution" plan. As the name suggests, instead of a guaranteed payout, participants and/or their employers contributed a specified amount that was then invested in stocks or other investments, with the returns determined by the market. In 1981 the IRS clarified the tax treatment of the 401(k) plan (named for the section of the tax code where it was covered), and the following year companies began to offer these plans to employees— first as a supplement, and eventually as an alternative to the defined benefit plan. Unlike DB plans, the 401(k) was owned by the employee and was portable, so that if they changed jobs they took the money with them. They were typically administered by an outside provider (e.g., Fidelity), and were instantly popular with employers.

According to data from the Economic Benefits Research Institute, 401(k) plans have almost entirely replaced traditional corporate pensions, which mostly linger among older employees in traditional industries. Proponents of the plans saw them as providing benefits to both employers and workers. Workers were not as tied to a single employer anymore, giving them the flexibility to move on as their career developed, and employers had a more straightforward and delimited commitment.

Yet the 401(k) plan has been, to put it gently, a miserable failure that is destined to leave many retirees in poverty. According to Teresa Ghilarducci: "Seventy-five percent of Americans nearing retirement age in 2010 had less than $30,000 in their retirement accounts. Almost half of middle-class workers, 49 percent, will be poor or near poor in retirement, living on a food budget of about $5 a day."[8]

How can this be? The need to save an adequate amount for retirement is surely something everyone realizes. Yet think back to your first day on the job, when someone from HR handed you a giant stack of folders and forms to fill out—one of which was your enrollment for a 401(k), offering you a large set of options that made no sense ("age-aggressive socially responsible balanced fund?"). You worked there for a couple of years, then you stopped out to go back to graduate school—borrowing against the value of your 401(k)—got another job with a similarly cryptic array of 401(k) options, worked as a 1099 contractor, partnered with a friend on a small startup, more freelance work, another corporate job, kids, college funds ... whatever happened to that 401(k) anyway? Like virtually everyone, you are not an expert in financial planning, and don't have time to research and update your options every time something changes in your life.

As Ghilarducci concluded, "It is now more than 30 years since the 401(k)/Individual Retirement Account model appeared on the scene. This do-it-yourself pension system has failed. It has failed because it expects individuals without investment expertise to reap the same results as professional investors and money managers. What results would you expect if you were asked to pull your own teeth or do your own electrical wiring?"

The changing face of the biggest employers

AFTER THE TREATY of Detroit, the cover charge for being a major corporation was fairly high. Companies were expected to provide stable, long-term employment with room for advancement, health insurance for employees and their families, and retirement pensions. As it happened, the American economy was poised for a long period of growth, and corporate employers in general were able to make good on those promises. A career with General Motors or Westinghouse or Eastman Kodak or Bethlehem Steel might not be exciting, but it was secure, and it did have benefits.

The biggest corporate employers today look very different than those in the postwar corporate heyday. In 1950, the biggest private employers were AT&T, General Motors, US Steel, General Electric, Sears, Bethlehem Steel, Ford, Chrysler, Standard Oil (Exxon), and Westinghouse. These were predominantly large manufacturers and technology firms with a long time horizon and employment practices to support it, including well-developed career ladders. The biggest private employers in 2010 were Walmart, Target, UPS, Kroger, Sears, Holdings AT&T, Home Depot, Walgreens, Verizon, and Supervalu. Nine of the 12 largest US employers today are in retail, where wages and benefits are modest at best, turnover is high, and career mobility extremely limited. Walmart alone has about as many US employees as the dozen largest manufacturers combined.[9] The career ladder at a Walmart store is more of a step stool, and benefits packages are not designed to encourage lifetime attachments.

The economic rationale for providing employee benefits was that companies and workers had a mutual interest in maintaining a long-term relationship when employees had specialized skills that made them particularly valuable. Of course, such companies still exist—perhaps Google, for instance, or a handful of other prominent technology employers that offer extravagant benefits to their (fairly tiny) workforces. In retail, however, skills are relatively generic, as demonstrated by the high level of annual turnover. If training for a job takes less than a day, employers have little reason to build an elaborate system of benefits to hang on to employees.

The other explanation for providing benefits was the power of labor. Industrial unions were at the apex of their power in the immediate postwar era, as the lengthy strikes in the auto, steel, and railroad industries demonstrated. In retail, however, unions struggle to gain and maintain a foothold, and the proportion of the private labor force that is unionized has declined continuously since the 1950s.

Commentators in the 1990s wrote about the "death of the career" as some of the trends we have discussed unfolded. Careers had devolved into jobs, with employees often moving from firm to firm, or working as independent contractors. In some industries, we are currently witnessing another shift: from jobs to tasks. Consider Uber, the ride-hailing platform. As of December 2014, Uber had roughly 2,000 employees but 162,000 "driver-partners" in the US.[10] (By contrast, GM is down to 120,000 employees in North America.) The company is careful to specify that these driver-partners are not employees (absolutely not!) but independent micro-entrepreneurs. They do not work for Uber: They work for themselves, and therefore have no claim on employee benefits, overtime, unemployment, or even a minimum wage. Amazon's Mechanical Turk (MTurk) is another platform that offers "Turkers" the chance to engage in "Human Intelligence Tasks" (HITs) for a piece rate determined by how much they bid. Again, this is not a job with Amazon: Amazon simply provides the platform for a market that matches those who have tasks to do with self-starters willing to do them.

It is not much of a leap to project that any task that has not been automated or outsourced, and that requires only minimal special- ized training, is subject to Uberization. Why should Walmart have "employees" (with their schedules and their craving for benefits) when it could instead provide a platform for micro-entrepreneurs recruited each day via a smartphone app? After all, "employees" expect a regular wage, while "partners" might be willing to bid against each other for tasks on a daily basis. (At the time of this writing, the status of Uber drivers as employees or independent contractors is under dispute.)

Conclusion

IN THE YEARS immediately following World War II, the US created a peculiar system of social welfare that relied on corporate employers to provide for health care and retirement income. At the time, some considered this to be an unseemly form of paternalism that would create dependence on the corporation, like serfs laboring at a feudal manor. Others considered social welfare functions to be the job of gov- ernment, not business. For better or worse, however, the US evolved an entire ecosystem of corporate benefits that ended up shaping the development of both the health care and financial services industries.

In retrospect, it is clear that this system was unsustainable. Corporations shouldered responsibilities that became increasingly costly over time, and that they were not especially suited for. What does a steel company know about health care? What does an oil company know about retirement planning? Moreover, this system created dynamics with broad implications beyond the corporation itself. The American health care system grew to be both astonishingly costly and surprisingly ineffective in large part because it was funded by dispersed corporate employers and fragmented insurance companies, abetted by a misguided tax system. As a nation, we are currently struggling our way to an alternative system that is less arbitrary and more cost effective. Our private pension system, primarily in the form of individually managed 401(k) plans, has been an abject failure, and it is reasonable to predict that baby boomers will be quite stretched in retirement, given their limited savings.

Meanwhile, many businesses have responded by doing whatever is necessary to avoid creating jobs directly. It's expensive to be a benevolent employer, providing health insurance and pensions. The standard employment package for the biggest employers in the postwar era is now out of reach for many. And while there are a few companies that provide lavish benefits in an effort to build long-term ties to employees, such as Google, they tend to be relatively small and rare. On the other hand, the biggest employers are in sectors with low wages, minimal benefits, and high turnover. Some recent success stories rely heavily on temporary and contract labor (e.g., Amazon); others attempt to eschew employment entirely (Uber).

Is there an alternative system that can provide social welfare benefits while providing a welcoming climate for business? Denmark provides one possibility. Its "flexicurity" system features generous social welfare benefits (funded by fairly high taxes) and a climate that encourages entrepreneurship by making it easy to start a business, and relatively painless to fail. Peer Hull Kristensen of Copenhagen Business School noted that every year 250,000 businesses fail in Denmark—and 260,000 new ones are started.[11] Freed of the demand to fund employment benefits (which are provided by the government to all citizens), firms can explore more speculative and risky possibilities. Potential employees don't have to worry that if the business fails, they will lose their family's health insurance or be unable to retire. Perhaps this system is impractical for the US. Yet it is ironic that a "nanny state" has turned out to be so adept at promoting entrepreneurship, while America has created so many obligations for corporate employers that the corporate form itself is dying off.

CHAPTER 10

RISING INEQUALITY

THE RISE OF the Occupy Wall Street movement in 2011 drew attention to vast inequities in the allocation of wealth and income in the United States. Activists and scholars pointed out that the 1% at the top was drawing ever farther away from the other 99%. An elite class of top executives, financiers, and wealthy heirs seemed to exercise disproportionate influence over America's economy and politics. Presidential hopefuls sought audiences with a handful of billionaires who had the ability to single-handedly finance electoral campaigns. How did we get to a point where fossil fuel magnates like the Koch Brothers, or a casino owner like Sheldon Adelson, are able to demand obedience to their peculiar preferences?

Many attribute the new inequality to the unbridled power of corporations. Through limitless political spending and ludicrously unbalanced compensation systems, corporations would seem to be the major cause of inequality in America today. Thanks to their eight- and nine-figure CEO salaries and their lavish political action funds, corporations maintain a system of stark inequality.

Yet as I argue in this chapter, it is not the surging power of corporations but their collapse that is causing increased inequality. The growth of large corporate employers in the postwar period corresponded to a substantial drop in inequality in the US. Corporations equalized compensation systems across the economy and provided career ladders that enabled individuals to move into the middle class. Conversely, as corporations adapted to the demands of maximizing shareholder value by contracting out their supply chains, and as retail replaced manufacturing as the largest source of employment, labor markets became increasingly polarized. The result has been the decline of employment by major corporations and a corresponding increase in income inequality.

Why is inequality going up?

INEQUALITY HAS INCREASED dramatically over the past generation, both within the US and around the world. The income of the top 1% in the US has grown far more than that of the other 99%, reaching levels of disparity not seen since the start of the Great Depression in 1929.[1] Between 1979 and 2007, after-tax income for the middle 60% increased 42%. For those in the top 1%, it more than tripled, and their take now amounted to over 20% of all income in the US.[2] The rise of CEO pay has been even more breathtaking. Whereas CEOs made 20 times as much as the average worker in 1965, in 2014 they made more than 300 times as much.[3] At a speech at Georgetown University in May 2015, President Obama pointed out that the top 25 hedge fund managers earned more than all kindergarten teachers in the US combined.[4] Things are even more skewed when it comes to wealth. The Walton family, heirs to the Walmart fortune, hold as much wealth as the bottom 40% of the American population put together.[5] We have clearly entered a new Gilded Age in which a small group is gaining fabulous wealth while the bulk of the population is stagnating financially.

But while almost everyone agrees that inequality has increased, they may not agree on what that means. What exactly is inequality? Inequality is pervasive in part because inequality can refer to so many things: Why is the 1% so much better off than the other 99%? Why do men earn more on average than women? Why do African Americans experience such different treatment from the authorities than whites? Why do dim-bulb children of the wealthy finish college at higher rates than gifted children from low-income families?

A first distinction is between income and wealth. Income is how much you earn in a given year; wealth is how much you have accumulated over time, or over generations. Wealth tends to be especially concentrated because families can hand it down from one generation to the next, giving each new generation a huge head start. Most of us inherit little or nothing from our parents, but the wealthy (like the Waltons) can inherit billions. Some discussions of inequality are more focused on poverty—that is, what accounts for how much of the population is below the poverty line. Others focus on mobility: Why are some able to move up, while others are not? Still other discussions are oriented around group differences: Why do women earn less than men on average? Why do whites earn more than blacks? Those on the political right often like to distinguish between equality of outcomes (which is easy to observe, and inequality is flagrant) and equality of opportunities (which is very hard to observe, but easy to advocate).

This chapter will focus on the distribution of incomes: how much people earn from their jobs (or other sources) each year, and how much that varies across the overall population The most common measure of distributional inequality is the Gini index. The Gini index ranges from zero (where everyone has exactly the same income) to one (where a single person has all the income). Notably, the Gini index measures not the level of income, but its distribution. In other words, the Gini does not measure how big the pie is, but how it is divided. It does not matter if the average income is $100 per year or $100,000 per year; the Gini simply measures how incomes vary across the population. And measured by the Gini index, income inequality in the US has gone up almost continuously since the 1980s.

The standard stories explaining increasing inequality often emphasize a combination of broad economic and technological trends and the choices of individuals. The popular recent version of this is the argument for "skill-biased technological change." When major technologies change, it often makes some kinds of skills less valuable and other kinds of skills more valuable. The growth of factory production made mechanical skills more valuable relative to agricultural skills, and inequality went up. The economist Simon Kuznets noticed in the 1950s that the level of income inequality seemed to be higher in newly industrializing economies than in either agricultural economies or advanced industrial economies, and hypothesized that advances in technology first increased inequality (as new skills and capital ownership become more valued), then decreased it, an idea summarized in the "Kuznets curve."

By this account, the spread of information and communication technologies (ICTs) have increased inequality by making some new skills (e.g., programming) especially valuable, while others (say, manual production labor) become less valuable. Presumably, the current round of increasing inequality is simply a blip on the road to a more equitable future, as more people abandon manufacturing and retail to learn programming languages such as Python and SQL (structured query language).

This story has some plausibility—we can all think of precocious kids who write an app in their dorm room and end up billionaires, or others who lost their jobs when the furniture factory closed or the Blockbuster went out of business. But the most unequal countries are not the most tech-savvy (for example, Zimbabwe, Peru), while some of the most advanced (for example, Japan, Germany) have relatively low inequality. Moreover, the big leaps in inequality have not corresponded to technological shocks in any obvious way. The UK's inequality increased enormously between the time Margaret Thatcher took office (1979) and the time she left (1990), but has been relatively flat since then, even as the World Wide Web spread information technology to every home and business.[6]

Alternatively, some emphasize the political power of the wealthy and their ability to mold public policy to favor their own interests. Thomas Piketty provides the most celebrated recent account, giving a long history of inequality in capitalist economies leading up to the current moment.[7] At bottom, Piketty's analysis compares the rate of return on investment (R)—which summarizes how much income goes to those who own investments—with the rate of growth of the economy over all (G). When R is greater than G (R > G), income tends to become more concentrated in the hands of the wealthy—that is, those whose incomes primarily come from investing rather than working (sometimes called "rentiers"). But how exactly do people end up getting paid differently? The idea that economy-wide forces, like skill-biased technological change or R > G, cause increased inequality is kind of like knowing that if you eat a lot of salt, your blood pressure will go up. It may be true, but we want to know how exactly this happens. Does it have anything to do with all those organs sitting inside our chest cavity?

Consider how people end up getting the salary they do. The vast majority of people work for organizations, often giant corporate employers like Walmart or General Motors. Thus, the processes that shape who gets what depend on organizations: how businesses come to hire particular people, how much they pay them, how they promote them (or not), how they fire them. Jobs and salaries are allocated by organizations. If we want to understand why people get paid what they do, we need to examine organizations and their pay practices.

How size matters

NOTHING CONVEYS INEQUALITY more clearly than a corporate hierarchy: the pyramid-shaped organization chart with the CEO at the top, the executive parking lot, the offices whose sizes and altitudes correspond to rank in the organization. Corporations exude rampant differences in status between the haves and the have-nots, which is why we frequently hear about the ratio of the CEO's salary to that of the average worker. For instance, the CEO-to-worker pay ratio for American Express is 119:1; for AT&T, 100:1; and for CVS Caremark, 422:1.[8]

Divergent salaries are built in to the structure of the corporation. Writing in the 1950s, Nobel Prize winner Herbert Simon noted that organizations in general had a norm that salaries of bosses and subordinates should be roughly proportional—perhaps bosses should earn 30% more than those who reported to them. Since people could only manage so many subordinates, this meant that as organizations grew bigger, their hierarchies grew taller, and those at the top earned more money.[9] This gave those at the top incentives to grow their organizations, even if it was not especially profitable to do so: bigger paid better.

At first blush, you might expect that economies with bigger corporations would suffer greater income inequality. If corporations are built to be unequal, and bigger corporations are more unequal than smaller ones, then an economy full of giant corporations should be particularly unequal. Yet the truth is precisely the opposite: The most equal economies (for example, the Scandinavian countries) are home to some of the biggest global corporations (Nokia, Volvo, Maersk, Ericsson, Statoil, Novo Nordisk, Ikea), while the most unequal economies (for example, Colombia, South Africa) have few if any truly large-scale domestic enterprises. In fact, as I discovered in research with Adam Cobb at the Wharton School, around the world there is a strong negative correlation between the proportion of the labor force employed by the biggest domestic corporations and the level of inequality. Countries with bigger corporate employers tend to experience lower economic inequality, and vice versa.[10]

Nowhere is the link between corporate size and income inequality more evident than in the United States. Figure 10.1 shows the trends over time in inequality (measured by the Gini index) and the proportion of the US workforce employed by the 10 biggest companies since 1950. Both have gone up and down over the years, but what is most

FIGURE 10.1   Income inequality and employment concentration in the United States, 1950–2006

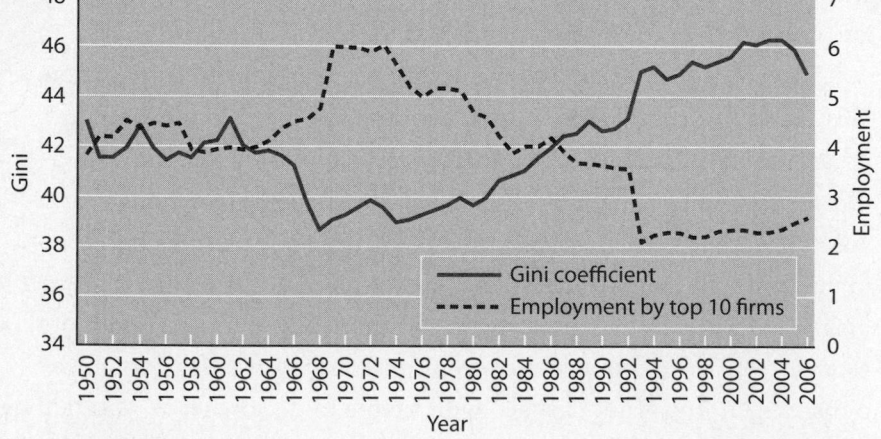

Source: Davis and Cobb, 2010

remarkable is the correlation: almost −0.9. In other words, inequality and employer size are almost mechanically linked. When companies grew bigger (such as in the 1960s), economic inequality went down; when companies shrunk (for example, during the takeover wave of the 1980s), inequality went up. If you are not a social scientist, let me emphasize that this correlation is really, really big. Weight and blood pressure are strongly correlated, but this is bigger than that.

How is this possible? If big firms are more unequal than small firms, then shouldn't economies composed of bigger firms be more unequal than small-firm economies? The connection is counterintuitive, but think of it this way. Imagine that General Motors has one million employees, with a wide range of compensation. The executives will be paid more than the middle managers, who will be paid more than the engineers, who will be paid more than the production workers, who will be paid more than the grounds crew. At the very top will be a well-paid CEO. Now imagine splitting GM up into 100 companies, each with its own CEO. We might have McKinsey-style consultants occupying the top office, a freestanding finance unit (in New York, not Detroit), a group of strategy consultants finding new ways to outsource, an IT contractor, an elite set of skilled tradespersons, vast assembly lines largely staffed by a temp agency, and an off-the-books grounds crew. Within each of these smaller groups compensation might be more equal, but across the 100 companies we are likely to see vast disparities in pay. The finance and IT and consulting people are certain to be much better paid outside GM; the temp assemblers will receive much lower compensation. Across the million employees, inequality is lower in GM-world than in contractor-world.

As Herbert Simon recognized long ago, the organization's boundaries are social boundaries. People compare salaries *within* companies to assess their fairness, but not so much *across* companies. Magazines frequently feature articles comparing CEO salaries to those of the average employee, yet we don't see articles comparing the salary of the head of a 25-person hedge fund shop in New York to those of the other people that work in their building. Salary differences within organizations seem highly relevant; those across organizations, not so much.

In our research, Adam Cobb and I labeled this the "paradox of hierarchy." The paradox is that although bigger corporations are more unequal internally than smaller ones, economies composed of bigger corporations tend to be more equal overall. It's not the only example of aggregate outcomes (e.g., national income inequality) being contrary to what you might expect from their components (e.g., corporate salary structures). As another example, consider the 2008 presidential election in the US. African Americans voted for President Obama at near-unanimous levels. You might therefore expect that states with the largest African American populations would be the places where Obama carried the biggest margins. Yet almost the opposite was true. Here are the five states with the largest black population percentages, and their votes for Obama's white opponent, John McCain: Mississippi (37%, 56%); Louisiana (32%, 59%); Georgia (31%, 52%); Maryland (39%, 37%); South Carolina (28%, 54%). In short, McCain won handily in four of the five states with the largest black populations.

A small history of corporate size in America

THE US IS currently experiencing a degree of inequality not seen since the Gilded Age of the late 19th century, when railroad barons were building vacation mansions in Newport and endowing universities like Stanford and Vanderbilt. Yet the period of America's most even income distribution was within living memory, in the late 1960s. What was it about the postwar era that promoted greater income equality, and what was it that changed to set us on our current path?

The most straightforward explanation is that unions were powerful enough after the war to negotiate favorable wage bargains, and that as unions gained members and power, inequality declined. Yet the union-ized proportion of the nonfarm labor force has been in almost contin-uous decline since the mid-1950s, when about one-third of workers were members of unions. As union density declined in the 1960s, so did inequality. Union power alone cannot explain these trends. There has been a surprising dance between corporate size and income inequality in the US (see Figure 10.1), with both moving up and down in seemingly unpredictable ways over time, but in patterns that were clearly connected to each other.

Commentators in the 1950s and 1960s pointed out that executive salaries tended to be strongly related to the size of the business they ran, but only minimally related to profits. As I noted earlier, Herbert Simon explained this by pointing out that social norms favored pro-portional salaries among bosses and subordinates. While "the market" might shape how much entry-level jobs paid, once someone started climbing the corporate ladder their pay depended on where they were in the hierarchy. Therefore, the bigger the company, the taller the hierarchy, and the greater the salary at the top. This gave those who ran corporations good reason to grow their business, and helps explain why executives seem to love making acquisitions, even when they frequently fail to pan out.

Pay alone was not the only thing that drove corporate growth. Size is also correlated with visibility and prestige. The Fortune 500 is not ranked by who is most profitable, but by who is biggest. Bigger firms had more power, taller headquarters, more impressive fleets of corporate jets. And growing firms provide more opportunities for their employees to move up the hierarchy. There were so many reasons to want to grow—why let profitability get in the way? By 1970, the 25 biggest American corporations employed the equivalent of over 10% of the private labor force. A few dozen corporations had grown so large that they were, to a large extent, the American labor market. Their policies determined who got hired, how much they got paid, and who moved up in the world.

But growth cannot go on forever. Beginning in the early 1980s, Wall Street and Washington eventually found a way to put an end to the days of limitless corporate growth. Rampant bust-up takeovers and the new mantra of corporate focus de-constructed the conglomerates back into their component parts, each of which evolved their own hiring and compensation practices. Moreover, those at the top were increasingly paid not for growth but for performance—specifically for creating shareholder value. The size that mattered now was not revenues but market capitalization. Employing large numbers of people was no longer a source of pride, but a sign that the CEO had not gotten the memo to be more like Neutron Jack, who ruthlessly downsized General Electric. As more elements of the corporate value chain became eligible for outsourcing, companies came to adopt the "virtual corporation" model (described in Chapter 6). Small was now beautiful; to be big was to be a dinosaur.

Conclusion: Small is beautiful …
if you love inequality

AS WE HAVE seen elsewhere in this book, corporate size and growth were rewarded for most of the postwar period in the US. Companies sought to grow revenues, assets, employment, and share price. There was reason to expect that a handful of corporations would eventually acquire all the rest, leaving too few corporations to fill the Fortune 500 list. Surprisingly, as corporations grew, inequality declined. At the high water mark of the "corporate century," during Richard Nixon's administration, inequality was at its lowest ebb in America.

Yet this situation has been almost entirely reversed. Nothing about the current corporate system favors becoming "large," least of all in employment: Technology and pressures to create shareholder value have led companies to be as tiny as possible, and to avoid long-term commitments to employees. The corporate *career*, with a series of jobs bearing more responsibility (and pay) was replaced by the *job*, and now the job is being replaced by the *task*.

Postwar critics saw the ever-growing corporate sector as a threat to democracy and the environment. In 1973, at the point when corporations were at their apex of concentration, E. F. Schumacher published *Small Is Beautiful: A Study of Economics as if People Mattered*. The phrase "small is beautiful" resonated widely. The environmental and social consequences of gearing the economy toward limitless growth were dire. Yet Schumacher gloomily concluded (in a chapter titled "Towards a Theory of Large-Scale Organization") that "nobody really likes large-scale organization. . . . Yet, it seems, large-scale organization is here to stay."[11]

Who would have guessed that we might someday lament the passing of the large-scale organization? Yet surprisingly enough, when it comes to greater income equality, big is beautiful. As we will see in the next chapter, those monster corporations also had something to recommend them when it came to providing economic opportunity.

CHAPTER 11

DECLINING UPWARD MOBILITY

A CENTRAL PART OF America's national identity is the idea that anyone who works hard and plays by the rules can move up in the world. Indeed, we are suspicious of those who are handed success rather than earning it through their own grit and determination. Presidential candidate Mitt Romney, whose father was the CEO of an auto company and governor of Michigan, attended an exclusive boarding school before getting degrees at Harvard Business School and Harvard Law School and running a private equity firm. But in her speech to the 2012 Republican National Convention that nominated Romney, his wife was compelled to describe their hardscrabble existence as newlyweds in a basement apartment, where they "ate a lot of pasta and tuna fish" and "our dining room table was a fold-down ironing board in the kitchen."

Yet politicians and commentators from across the political spectrum now lament Americans' stagnant incomes and declining upward mobility. Recent college graduates find themselves working as baristas or cobbling together part-time jobs with no benefits in order to pay off their student loans. Those with cars might become self-employed "micro-entrepreneurs" driving for Uber. Even the last-ditch option of the liberal arts graduate is no longer viable: Law school enrollments in 2014 were down 40% from 4 years earlier, and only 57% of the class of 2013 ended up in jobs that required passing the bar.[1] And things are far worse for the working class without a college degree, where incomes have been stagnant for a generation and the prospects for substantial income growth nearly absent.

In this chapter I argue that upward mobility in the United States in the postwar years was underwritten by the large corporation. Corporations provided entry-level jobs with room for moving up. Their stability and growth meant that a corporate career was secure; their tall hierarchies meant that there was a clear path upward. But as corporations recede in importance, pathways to upward mobility become harder to navigate. Careers were replaced by jobs, and now jobs are being replaced by tasks. We have entered a chutes-and-ladders economy in which a few gain riches through a seemingly random process, while others muddle through.

How to join the middle class

WHAT ADVICE WOULD you give to a 17-year-old heading out into the big world today? High school graduation speakers confront this problem every year around June. With rare exceptions, their advice—believe in yourself, work hard, follow your dreams—is anodyne and supremely unhelpful. Suppose a niece or nephew asked for your sincere guidance about how they should make their way in the world. They are reasonably smart, personable, digital natives. You sense that they would like to reach age 35 with a reliable income, little or no debt, and the prospect of having enough resources to own a home and raise a family. Optimistically, they might also want to be a bit better off than their parents. What would go into your how-to guide?

For the first four decades after World War II, there was a nearly foolproof recipe to achieve a solid middle-class life. First, study hard, get good grades in high school, and aim to attend the most prestigious college you can. An Ivy League school is great, but a flagship public university will do fine, and could be largely funded through summer jobs. College graduates historically had low unemployment rates and higher compensation than nongraduates, so as an investment decision, going to college was an easy call.

Second, major in something practical. Subjects such as engineering, accounting, or computer science are safe bets, providing skills that are always in demand. (Of course, if you major in something frivolous like philosophy or English literature, as I did, there's always law school.)

Third, with your degree in hand, get a job with a name-brand corporation in an industry with good growth prospects. Big firms are secure and provide the most opportunities for advancement. Peter Drucker wrote in 1949, "Where only 20 years ago the bright graduate of the Harvard Business School aimed at a job with a New York Stock Exchange house, he now seeks employment with a steel, oil, or automobile company."[2] The more adventurous might consider IBM, or even Xerox.

Fourth, buy the biggest and most costly house you can afford. Houses always go up in value, and the tax code favors home ownership. There is no safer investment than an American home.

Fifth, make sure your employer has a solid pension plan. If you can, put your kids' college funds and additional retirement savings into a diversified mutual fund. Over the long run, the market always goes up, and the stock market beats all the alternatives for investment returns.

Finally, your reward: a comfortable retirement in Florida.

The path to upward mobility almost inevitably led through the corporate world. Companies like Eastman Kodak or Westinghouse or AT&T or General Motors were big and growing. The room for advancement from an entry-level job was almost limitless. And although life as the man in the gray flannel suit might not be as exciting as the makers of *Mad Men* would imply, it was secure.

What happened to upward mobility?

IN RECENT YEARS, politicians on both the left and the right have fretted that economic mobility is not what it used to be. Those who work hard and play by the rules ought to be able to earn a comfortable living, buy a house, help send their kids to college, and retire with some security and dignity. But the rules seem to have changed. Jobs have replaced careers, houses turn out to be a risky investment, college costs have surged beyond the means of average families, and when kids get out of college they often wind up in dead-end jobs that could be filled by high school grads. (Skim milk, extra shot.) Given the state of the typical 401(k), retirement is a dream beyond the horizon for many.

Studies show that upward mobility in the US is not nearly as high as people might have thought. The land of Horatio Alger bears more resemblance to the land of Charles Dickens. Like inequality, mobility can be defined in different ways. "Intergenerational mobility" refers to whether we are better or worse off than our parents. Mobility researchers might ask how much a man earns at age 40 compared to what his father earned at that age. Looking at whether those who start at the bottom move up is especially instructive. What proportion of those who grew up in the bottom 20% were still in the bottom 20% as adults? Conversely, what proportion made it into the top 20%? These kinds of figures are useful because they can be compared across countries and over time.

Here, the situation belies the story of America as a land of opportunity. One recent study found that 42% of American men raised in the bottom 20% stayed there as adults, while only 8% made it into the top 20%. These figures were far worse than in Western Europe and Scandinavia, suggesting that those at the low end in the US were more stuck than is widely known.[3] The rags-to-riches stories that Americans love turn out to be not so common in practice. How much this has changed in recent generations is subject to debate. One study found that young men who entered the labor force in the 1980s and 1990s were more than twice as likely to stay in low-wage, dead-end jobs for the next decade compared with similar men who joined the workforce in the late 1960s and early 1970s, at the high point of the corporate economy.[4] On the other hand, some new research suggests that intergenerational mobility in the US has been low for decades.[5] It is likely that mobility patterns vary depending on where one starts; in any case, it appears that perceptions may finally be catching up to reality.

Other research examines what kinds of jobs are growing and declining in prevalence, which gives a glimpse into future mobility. For many years the labor market has been described as polarized, with most of the growth coming in low-skilled jobs (e.g., in retail, cleaning, food service, security). But there was also growth in well-paid jobs demanding high levels of skill and training. Meanwhile, middle-skill jobs have been in decline due to automation and offshoring. Yet the optimistic note at the high end of the labor market may be fading. One recent study found that college graduates enjoyed greater opportunities for higher-skilled "cognitive jobs" in the 1990s, but this reversed after 2000.[6] This might help account for why mobility seems to have dropped more than figures indicate. Perhaps the most recent college cohorts are graduating into a less rewarding labor market than those who came before, which may limit their future mobility. (One sign of this is that nearly half of Uber drivers have college degrees.) Other research examines the trajectories of individuals and how much their income grew (or declined) over time. This work is often summarized in terms of how many different jobs people can be expected to have by age 40.

As our how-to guide hinted, the golden era of economic opportunity in the US was largely made possible by the large corporation. In Chapter 10, I described the "paradox of hierarchy," by which big, hierarchical corporations helped reduce inequality at the level of the economy. Corporate hierarchies are starkly unequal, with endless status gradations from the mailroom in the basement to the CEO's corner office on the top floor. Viewed in this way, the collapse of corporate hierarchies might be seen as a victory for human equality.

Yet one person's status hierarchy is another person's career ladder (at least if that person is male, white, and unburdened by the demands of child care). The idea of working your way up from the mailroom to the executive suite only makes sense within an organizational hierarchy. Corporations provided a stable institution, separate from the uncertainty of the market, with well-marked pathways to move up. The stability and growth of the corporate sector is what made the investment of going to college such a safe bet. Most of the blue chip companies listed in the Dow Jones Index in 1930 were still there 60 years later. Corporate careers were bland and predictable. The biggest risk of going to work at Bethlehem Steel or Union Carbide was not economic security but boredom.

Those without a college education also benefited economically from the corporate system. From Henry Ford's $5 workday to the Great Migration that allowed African Americans to escape the Jim Crow south to wage employment in the north, big corporations provided opportunity for all skill levels. Both of my grandfathers, lacking formal education and any relevant prior training, found economic mobility by moving to Detroit to work in the big car factories. The working class was elevated en masse into the middle class in large part thanks to large corporate employers.

From career to job to task

THE COLLAPSE OF big corporate employers means that we no longer have a legible map for upward mobility. In the 1990s commentators began to write about the "death of the career." Corporations might still provide jobs, but they would no longer provide job ladders. As Jack Welch of GE put it, companies would not offer extended employment, but instead employability. In other words, working at GE meant that you would not have a hard time finding work somewhere else.[7]

The notion of an entry-level job implies that it is the first rung on a ladder. But today many positions are what used to be called "dead-end jobs," with few places to move up. A job in the mailroom is no longer "entry level" if the mailroom is run by a contractor or temp agency. And even getting into the mailroom in the first place might be a prize. Tens of thousands of workers are hired by temp services firms each year to staff Amazon warehouses. For a select few, the reward for outstanding performance is an actual dead-end job with Amazon.

For some industries, such as publishing, film, fashion, and politics, the "pre-job" job pays nothing at all, and is known as an internship. Indeed, many college students are required to pay to receive college credit doing menial tasks because such internships are the cover charge to be considered for an entry-level job with actual compensation.[8]

In many sectors today, even a *job* is too great a commitment. Instead, the job is being replaced by the *task*: doing specified pieces of work (driving someone to the airport, tagging objects in online photos) for specified compensation—not as an employee, but as a freestanding contractor. Uber, the ride-hailing platform, is the most prominent example of this new form of work. Thanks to the fact that much of the population carries a smartphone with GPS, Uber and similar platforms make it possible for consumers to contract for microwork (walking a dog, picking up groceries, wrapping gifts, watering plants) for a set fee. In some cases, potential contractors bid against each other to offer the lowest rate. At Amazon's MTurk, for instance, this dynamic ensures that many Turkers routinely earn less than the minimum wage. Because they are not employees, but rather freestanding micro-entrepreneurs, the minimum wage does not apply.

This new form of "platform capitalism" (a more accurate term than "sharing economy") is highly likely to spread to any kind of task that can be easily specified, at least if the law allows it. Note that skill per se is not a barrier to using this format: Platforms can require that their micro-entrepreneurs document their qualifications (say, a commercial driver's license, or a shelf-stocking certificate, or a medical degree).

The rapid global expansion of Uber, in spite of vehement opposition from taxi drivers and governments, shows the potential of platform capitalism to reshape both industries and the nature of the employment relation, a topic we take up in Chapter 13. The platform-capitalism model seems certain to spread widely, given its cost advantages. And it is not hard to imagine this model encroaching on retail and other employment. Might Walmart decide to offer certifications for various tasks and open them up to platforms on an as-needed basis? Why not dispense with set wage rates and allow pay to vary with demand each day? Why not create competitions for day-work that go to the lowest bidder, like MTurk? This might not be compatible with current employment law, but of course laws are not set in stone. As should be obvious, the possibilities for upward mobility in a world of tasks looks different from that in a world of jobs or careers.

The "chutes-and-ladders" labor market

NEARLY EVERY ELEMENT of the old rule book no longer applies. First, does it still make sense to go to college? The received wisdom is: obviously yes. College grads earn much more on average than nongrads, and their unemployment rates are substantially lower. Yet critics have pointed out that some of the most successful billionaire entrepreneurs of recent times—Bill Gates, Steve Jobs, Mark Zuckerberg—were college dropouts. Meanwhile, outstanding student loan debt was nearly $1.2 trillion at the end of 2014—more than auto loans and credit card debt. Peter Thiel, a cofounder of PayPal, even started a fellowship program in 2011 to offer 20 lucky young people $100,000 to skip college and start a business instead.[9] Of course, given the low success rate of startups, it is not obvious that this is a superior choice.

Second, will corporate employers reward your choice of high-value major? College is often discussed as an investment in human capital (although to outsiders it often looks more like consumption than investment). A degree at a good state school can cost more than $100,000—far more than the median baby boomer has saved for retirement. What should our 17-year-old study to equip himself or herself for a remunerative long-term career? Almost everyone would agree that a degree in computer science should be a bulletproof credential in the new economy. The world is in flux thanks to the relentless expansion of software into every area of the economy, but surely the programmers will survive. Yet in June 2015, the *New York Times* published an article describing how Disney planned to replace 250 IT workers with low-cost temps imported from India on H-1B visas. The laid-off workers were given a bonus if they stayed for the full 90 day transition; for many, that meant training their own replacements.[10]

The article provoked a substantial public outcry. Employers sometimes complain of a "skills gap," but this story suggested that the problem was a wage gap: Disney evidently did not want to continue paying American-sized wages to their programmers when there were cheaper alternatives. An online commentator named Maureen O'Brien identified an essential issue: "Who in their right mind is going to invest tens of thousands and years of training to get a job that will never develop into a lucrative career?"[11] If education is thought of as an investment, then corporate hiring practices help define the payoff for that investment. And if companies are quick to replace skilled workers with lower-cost replacements, then the alleged skill gap is likely to become a self-fulfilling prophecy. Who is going to invest in developing a skill when the payoff depends on the arbitrary actions of corporate employers?

Third, will your investment in an index fund pay off? Over the long run, the stock market has been a good investment, and it is impossible to predict what the future will bring. But there have been quite extended periods in which the market has been a problematic bet: The S&P 500 was 40% lower the day George W. Bush left office than the day he arrived. And if the trends in de-listings and IPOs continue, and alternative mechanisms for channeling capital continue to flourish, the market may not be able to bear the aspirations of all those prospective retirees.

Perhaps we are looking in the wrong place for career opportunities. Maybe young people don't want to work for a traditional 20th-century corporation. What about the high-tech economy? One survey of college graduates under 40 revealed that their top three preferred employers were Google, Apple, and Facebook.[12] Of course, the odds of landing a good job at any of these companies are quite slim. Nearly 1.9 million people graduated from college with a bachelor's degree in 2015. Facebook hired only 1,200 people globally in 2014, and planned to hire 1,200 more in 2015. (Notably, only 7 of their new hires were black, bringing the total to 45.[13]) Google had 53,600 employees at the end of 2014 and 47,756 in 2013, a net increase of less than 6,000. It reputedly receives 2 million applications per year, suggesting that one's odds of getting a job at Google may be as low as 3 in 1,000. And while Apple has 92,000 employees, half work in its retail stores, where pay is relatively low (under $12 per hour as recently as 2012) and career ladders limited.[14] The modal job at Apple is not a high-end software engineer but a sales clerk in a blue t-shirt at the mall.

Of course, corporations may not be the place to look for mobility in the tech industry. It is entrepreneurs who reap the greatest rewards—not those who work for Apple, but those who write ingenious apps for the iPhone. There are 1.5 million apps for sale on Google Play, and almost as many on the Apple App Store. Apple reports several hundred thousand registered developers. Is this where the real wealth is being created? There are some vivid success stories: The creators of WhatsApp, a texting application, sold their business to Facebook for roughly $20 billion. There are a handful of others who have made huge fortunes by writing and selling their apps at just the right moment, and they become the stuff of legend. But the numbers indicate that relatively few people are earning a living writing apps, much less retiring on their winnings before they reach drinking age.

The *New York Times* described two high school kids who had written an app to combat procrastination, which quickly became the best-selling productivity app on iTunes. The pair attended industry conferences and took meetings with heavyweights. Unfortunately, app development and marketing came at the expense of schoolwork and grades. The payoff? A total of $30,000 for the two of them (after Apple's cut, but before expenses for attending those industry conferences).[15] It is a safe bet that if high school kids can write best sellers, this is not an industry that will yield a reliable income. And while the Bureau of Labor Statistics projected that employment for software developers would increase from 521,000 in 2010 to 665,000 in 2020, this is hardly a bonanza.

In some sense, app entrepreneurship has a lot in common with professional sports, or drug dealing: The very high payoffs available to a small handful of winners ends up luring a lot of participants into a game that they are extremely unlikely to win. Echoing *Freakonomics*, we might ask "Why do app developers still live with their moms?" Because in a winner-takes-all economy, a handful of players get the bulk of the rewards, while most are left behind.[16]

The rules for moving up in the current economy are inscrutable. Remember the children's board game "Chutes and Ladders"? Players roll a die and move their game piece forward from square 1 to square 100 in a race. On some spaces, players are shown doing a good deed (reading a book, mowing the lawn) and they move up a ladder; on others they do bad deeds (gorging on candy, pulling someone's hair) and slide down a chute. Although the game was meant to convey lessons about good behavior, astute children realized that their fate did not depend on their choices, but on the throw of the die.

Today's labor market looks a lot like chutes and ladders. Some people stay in school, study computer science, get a job at a major American corporation (say, Disney), and find themselves unemployed after training their replacements. Others drop out of school after writing Facebook in their dorm room and wind up billionaires. Some people write good-enough apps in the early days of the iPhone and get rich. Others write essentially identical apps, and earn nothing.

Conclusion

FOR MUCH OF the 20th century, Americans could reasonably expect to be better off than the previous generation. Average incomes rose over time, and workers could expect to see their individual fortunes improve over the course of their career. The ambitious had a well-marked path to moving up in the world.

This system was underwritten by the corporate economy. Through their hiring practices and their internal job ladders, corporate employers created a legible career map. It was not open to everyone equally, by any means. But the corporate system did have its own form of meritocracy, and it could be held to account for discriminatory practices. As corporate employers have declined, careers have been replaced with jobs, and jobs are being replaced with tasks. The notion of a career ladder is increasingly out of sync with reality, where forces beyond our control seem to determine our fate. We now live in a chutes-and-ladders economy in which the connection between effort and outcomes is often obscure.

In the next chapter, we consider some of the bright spots of this new postcorporate system.

CHAPTER 12

SILVER LININGS

THE FIRST THREE chapters for Part III highlighted some of the negative social outcomes of the disappearing public corporation. The social safety net that was held aloft by corporate employers is falling apart; inequality is going up; mobility is going down. Should we be nostalgic for the dominance of corporations? Should we be trying to bring them back?

In this chapter I describe some of the silver linings of corporate decline. The technological and other changes that are making corporations less sustainable are opening up space for new alternatives that may not look like "organizations" at all. The costs of enabling people to collaborate on a large scale have drastically declined over the past three decades, and noncorporate alternatives are flourishing. Linux and Wikipedia demonstrate that it is possible for thousands of people dispersed around the world to produce amazing products for free; indeed, the Internet would barely be functional without the products of such open-source collaborations. The widespread adoption of smartphones has enabled "platforms" to match drivers and riders (like Uber) and other person-to-person transactions. These platforms need not be organized as corporations: Unlike railroads, they require little capital investment. We are also witnessing the early stages of low-cost, locally distributed manufacturing that will allow designs from anywhere in the world to be produced in our own neighborhood. Thanks to the emergence of all these new technologies that allow novel combinations, the variety of new ways of doing business is staggering.

Corporations will continue to prevail in some sectors. Oil refining, jet manufacturing, railroads, and infrastructure require large-scale investment in long-lived assets; these and some other industries will continue to be corporate. But they will seem somewhat vestigial, like the royal families that still live on in the UK and Denmark even after feudalism is long gone.

Misplaced nostalgia?

FOR OVER A century, "corporate" has been an epithet, and Progressives and others have lamented the concentration of economic power that the public corporation brings. Teddy Roosevelt concluded that gigantic corporations were a necessary evil: necessary, because bigger was cheaper; evil, because executives and bankers who owed no duty to the public, but only to their shareholders, had amassed so much power that they threatened our very democracy. The new corporations were producing huge fortunes for the few but little for the many. The new corporate elites seemed destined to create a new form of hereditary aristocracy. Meanwhile, future Supreme Court Justice Louis Brandeis in 1914 showed in his essays that shadowy financial elites were pulling the strings behind the economy through their powerful social networks.

The diagnosis of the Progressives sounds shockingly contemporary. Unrestrained corporate power, rampant inequality, unaccountable financial elites, politics corrupted by big money: Roosevelt and Brandeis could have been rocking the people's microphone at the Occupy movement in Zuccotti Park.

It therefore seems odd to claim that corporate decline could be anything but a blessing. I have argued that our current round of growing inequality and decreasing mobility are not due to corporate dominance, as in the Progressive Era, but its collapse. Am I suggesting we should revive the days of the mind-numbing assembly line and the even more mind-numbing three-martini lunch? Did peasants look back wistfully on the days of feudalism when they were freed from serfdom?

Economic transitions are hard, and their consequences can benefit some and harm others. The transition from feudalism to market capitalism entailed massive social upheaval as old understandings were cast aside. Few would advocate a return to feudalism, but we should not underestimate the challenges ahead as we survey some of the possibilities.

A Cambrian explosion of new forms

WHAT WOULD ORGANIZATIONS look like if funding them were not an issue? What if the costs of enabling people to collaborate on a grand scale—formerly the domain of governments and corporations—were dramatically lowered? This is the situation we are in now. The first 15 years of the new century have already seen an explosion of new forms, many of them noncorporate, enabled by new technologies, in particular the World Wide Web, that drastically lower the cost of collaboration. Books and movies that were science fiction when they were released (say, *Minority Report*) end up looking like documentaries a few years later. What if everyone carried a device that provided them with instant access to all the world's knowledge and the means to connect or collaborate with anyone else in the world instantaneously, for free? Right: iPhone + Wikipedia + Facebook. Things that would have seemed miraculous are quickly demoted to mundane. The implications of this new situation are endless, but here I want to focus on one: The cost of collaborating has gone down so low as to be largely inconsequential.

People are sometimes asked, "How would you live your life if you didn't have to work for a living?" We are now facing the organizational equivalent of this question: How would you organize if organizing were effectively free? The vanguard of this new movement for noncorporate alternatives happened in software, where activists have long promoted a norm of publishing free and open-source software, available to anyone who cared to use it. The Web depends overwhelmingly on such free software. According to Harvard law professor Yochai Benkler:

> Free and open source software programs account for roughly three-quarters of web servers, the software that a server runs to respond to browser queries (Apache; nginx); more than 70 percent of web browsers (Firefox, Chrome); server-side programming languages (PHP alone is >75 percent share);

content management systems (Wordpress, Joomla, and Drupal have slightly more than 70 percent of servers); all the way to enterprise stock management or statistical software, R. The sheer scale of our networked information economy's dependence on free software is staggering.[1]

Hundreds of millions of computers and phones run versions of the Linux operating system, including air traffic control systems, banks, and nuclear submarines. You can download it for free right now (search for "free linux download"). Yet Linux was not created by a corporation or government, but a dispersed group of thousands of programmers who have never been in the same place together. Based on the market's own test, software produced by a working anarchy easily beats software produced by corporations.

The same form of dispersed collaboration also produced the world's greatest amalgamation of knowledge, Wikipedia. When Wikipedia was launched in 2001 with a few dozen stubs for articles, it would have been impossible to imagine that it would grow within a few years to be the world's most used repository of knowledge. Access was free, and articles were written and edited entirely by anonymous unpaid volunteers. It was obviously doomed to fail. No sane person would have expected Wikipedia to work. Yet a decade later it is the über-encyclopedia that never stops expanding. By any reasonable standard, Wikipedia is a miracle. Corporations and governments did not do this (and their involvement is generally unwelcome). Wikipedia demonstrates that it is possible to engage the voluntary efforts of millions of people to produce great things without a centralized authority in charge. As Benkler puts it, "Over the course of the first decade of the twenty-first century, commons-based peer production has moved from being ignored, through being mocked, feared, and regarded as an exception or intellectual quirk, to finally becoming a normal and indispensable part of life."

But maybe software and online products like Wikipedia are different. Perhaps the kinds of distributed collaboration we can do sitting at a keyboard will not translate to the real world. Here again we are seeing some of the early days of an explosion in new forms. The smart-phone only came on the market in 2007, yet it has already enabled the creation of many new industries. Ride-hailing apps like Uber and Lyft were an almost instant success with consumers, and as discussed in previous chapters, Uber (founded in 2009) had more drivers in the United States in 2015 than GM (founded in 1908) had employees in North America. In recent years there has been a tsunami of new business startups tapping the basic insight that when almost everyone has a smartphone with a GPS, it is easy to create platforms allowing them to sell each other goods and services. The platform is almost inevitably pitched as "Uber for . . . ," and almost inevitably available first in San Francisco. There is an Uber for groceries, packages, flower delivery, on-street valet parking, laundry, medical marijuana, pizza, massage therapy, and physician house calls.[2] For any vaguely plausible service that one person is willing to do for another for money, someone in California is launching an Uber for that. (Go ahead: Think of the app, then search for it online. It's been done.)

Platform capitalism (a more accurate term than "the sharing economy") is at an early stage and could go in many directions. At this writing, Uber is under fire for classifying drivers as independent con-tractors rather than employees. The underlying legal question has yet to be fully resolved. In any case, it is not clear that "corporate plat-forms" will inevitably prevail. Critics such as Juliet Schor have pointed out that platforms don't necessarily add a lot of value themselves, and so Uber could be replaced by, say, worker-owned cab collectives.[3] Microsoft arguably lost out to Linux; AOL lost out to a free Web. Perhaps Uber and its ilk will lose out to open-source platform software.

All of the examples so far have been in the service industry, broadly construed: software, online content, mobile service platforms. Does any of this apply to manufacturing? In Chapter 7 I mentioned in passing that the cost of capital equipment, such as CNC (computer numerical control) machine tools, had been dropping drastically over the past 20 years. This sounds obscure, but is highly consequential. Fifty years ago printing documents in color required a large budget and the services of professional print shops staffed by specialized tradesmen. Thirty years ago a color laser printer might have cost $10,000, and only businesses or the very well-off could afford them. Today a color printer costs under $200. Now anyone with a PC can publish beautiful documents that they designed, with minimal skill, using readily available software. This is possible in large part because software has taken over the part of document production after you click "Print." Similarly, producing and distributing music no longer requires a studio and a record company: a laptop and Wi-Fi will do.

Consider the possibilities if capital equipment (the machines that create manufactured products, like routers for wood or milling machines for metal) followed the same technological development and downward cost trajectory as laser printers. This is what has been happening with CNC. We are reaching a point where it will be possible to equip every town with universal fabrication facilities using low-cost computerized equipment. "Universal" is a bit of an overstatement— your local makerspace is probably not equipped to produce a jet engine just yet. But a car may be not that far off.

We have seen that Nikefication has already separated design from production in many parts of the "manufacturing" sector. It is not hard to imagine that low-cost on-demand production facilities will end up "reshoring" much of manufacturing. The music-buying public long ago abandoned buying physical CDs in favor of iTunes. Why not buy furniture the same way? That is, why not buy designs from the world's best designers and have them fabricated at the local makerspace?[4] This is the theory behind Anne Filson and Gary Rohrbacher's AtFab, which provides beautiful designs from their studio in Kentucky that can be downloaded, customized, and fabricated anywhere out of whatever materials the customers want. As their website puts it, "An entirely digital process, from design to distribution to fabrication, eliminates the energy-intensive waste of global shipping, dispenses with mid-dlemen, and creates local manufacturing jobs. . . . Comprised of simple, flat interlocking parts, every piece in the collection can be cut from any off-the-shelf sheet material by a CNC machine, and assembled with basic, readily-available hardware."[5] The files are open source and it requires only modest skill to assemble the furniture.

It is easy to see how this model of fully separating design and fabrication might allow IKEA to get out of the manufacturing and distribution business entirely and just sell their designs. Much of their catalogue could already be produced with a $20,000 router and a few other machines, and designs could be optimized for freestanding fabrication. But it is also easy to see that open-source collaborative designs might end up replacing proprietary corporate designs entirely—think of Linux and Wikipedia. In 2014 the nonprofit Mozilla Foundation released a design for a $25 smartphone aimed at emerging markets that would use its open-source Firefox operating system.[6] It was not nearly as fancy as an iPhone, but it was far less costly. This initial shot across the bow was not a raging success, but it did demonstrate the possibility for noncorporate alternative designs.

It is still early days. One thing is clear: We are in the midst of a massive expansion of new forms of organizing the creation and delivery of goods and services, and it is not at all clear that the corporation will win out. Just as Progressivism shaped the development of the corporation in the first half of the 20th century, it is almost certain that political movements will shape our emerging economic system, for better or worse. We take up this question in the next chapter.

Where corporations will persist

THERE ARE MANY areas in which corporations will no longer be the most economical format for doing business. Yet there are also domains in which—for the time being—large scale seems inescapable. In these areas, corporations are likely to persist. The argument of this book has been that the corporation is especially suited to a particular 20th-century form of business. Public corporations make sense when there are risks, economies of scale (bigger is cheaper), and the expectation of a reasonably long time horizon. If the risks are small, then banks may be willing to fund the enterprise. If there are no economies of scale, then smaller enterprises funded by families or small investors make sense. If the venture is going to be short-lived, then it does not justify the transaction costs of going public. Railroads fit this description in the 19th century; mass production manufacturing fit it in the 20th. If technologies change to reduce economies of scale or the time horizon of a venture, then going public may not be the most economical option. I have argued that this has become true in many different industries.

But some activities still require massive scale and resources. We are unlikely to see locally brewed petroleum any time soon, or open-source jumbo jets produced in makerspaces. ExxonMobil—one of the successors of the Standard Oil Company, first created in 1870—may have achieved the corporate equivalent of eternal life (perhaps rivaled only by General Electric). As long as the world demands petroleum, and as long as the American people remain averse to state ownership of business enterprises, oil companies are highly likely to remain corporate entities. Railroads also require capital for land, tracks, track maintenance, and rolling stock that cannot be easily reduced through open-source software or clever phone apps. Aircraft production also requires capital on a large enough scale to make noncorporate (and nongovernmental) alternatives implausible.

Some forms of infrastructure will remain corporate for the immediate future, but may be challenged ultimately. At the moment, telephone networks seem to fit the criteria for requiring public corpo-rations. All those copper wires underground require capital to install and maintain. But of course landlines have been increasingly replaced by cellular telephones, where the idea of "long distance" seems quaint. And with Wi-Fi increasingly available, it is possible that traditional cellular telephones will be replaced by Wi-Fi phones. Why pay AT&T or Verizon for phone service if you have access to Facetime and texting apps for free? Similarly, cable television seems like an impregnable source of monopoly profits, and a good bet for remaining in the hands of public corporations. But if community-owned wireless mesh networks become a viable source of high-speed Internet access, then consumers may be able to disintermediate their cable provider entirely. With a $25 Mozilla phone, a $200 laptop, and a low-cost community wireless service, many households may be able to do without cable and telephone service. The generation that has never had a landline phone or a "long-distance" telephone service provider may be quite comfortable connecting with a Wi-Fi phone app, putting strains on the business models of telecom and cable companies.

Finally, the cost and performance of solar panels and home batteries will eventually reach a point where the neighborhood power grid may be able to replace the local electric utility (and perhaps even oil companies). It will not happen by 2018, but it might well happen.

Goodbye Wall Street

THERE IS ONE other possible silver lining in this story about the decline of the public corporation: It may also herald the decline of Wall Street. Whether this seems like a good thing or a bad thing will depend on the reader. Perhaps no other country on earth has made financial markets as central to their economy and their society as the United States. The US has traditionally had far more corporations listed on stock markets than other countries (although India surpassed the US in 2009 after the market collapse, and Japan is close). The market capitalization of listed companies in the US is routinely larger than its gross domestic product (GDP) (see Figure 12.1). The US also has an unusually large

FIGURE 12.1 Stock market capitalization as percentage of GDP, 2000

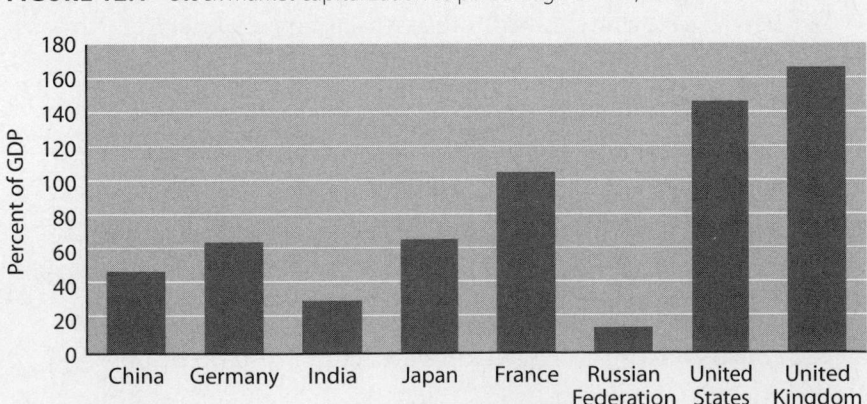

Source: Data from World Bank *World Development Indicators*

part of its population invested in the market. In few other places on earth are the market's movements as closely followed as in the US.

One reason for the centrality of financial markets is the peculiar history of the American corporation. As described earlier in this book, mass production for a continent-wide market meant that businesses had large capital needs that were most easily met by listing shares. But another reason America's financial markets are peculiar is the historical division of financial institutions into "commercial banking" and "investment banking." Commercial banks traditionally took in deposits and made loans to businesses. Investment banks underwrote stocks and bonds, making them available for sale on the financial markets.

In much of the industrialized world, and in the US today, the big banks that worked with major businesses were universal banks. In the US, however, particularly after the Glass-Steagall Act of 1933, the two types of banks were strictly separated. "Wall Street" proper largely consisted of freestanding investment banks that could underwrite securities (stocks and bonds) but could not make loans. Meanwhile, banking regulations meant that every major city had one or more local commercial banks. These banks could make loans, but they could not underwrite securities. This situation held until the repeal of Glass-Steagall in 1999, prompted in part by the merger of Citibank and Travelers (which included the Salomon Brothers investment bank).

By having a separate industry focused on financial markets, this division created a constituency for financial market-based solutions. A German universal banker might tell the board of a major business that sought capital, "We can make you a loan, or we can underwrite a bond issue. Let's see which is best." But an American banker could only do one of those. It is somewhat analogous to patients who seek advice about medical treatment from a surgeon. Surgeons are skilled at one type of treatment, but might not be as versed in the alternatives. Similarly, investment bankers were likely to be predisposed to market-based treatments.

For much of the 20th century, investment banking was heavily regulated and operated much like a utility, with a compensation system to match. The Reagan-era reforms described in Part II created a reinforcing cycle in which Wall Street and financial markets became richer and more powerful. By the 1990s, investment bankers filled many crucial positions in the Executive Branch, from Treasury Secretary on down. Unsurprisingly, they tended toward policies that were deferential to the financial markets. (Of course, there have been occasions to rethink this enthusiasm, notably in 2000 and 2008.)

But if access to funding is no longer a constraint—if the capital required to do business is systematically lower, and companies can safely avoid going to the markets for capital—then Wall Street becomes less essential. We have already seen that the number of IPOs has never recovered its level from the 1990s. In spite of the JOBS Act and numerous other inducements, businesses are finding good reasons to stay private and avoid the stock market entirely. The *New York Times* quoted Danielle Morrill, CEO of a startup called Mattermark: "If you can get $200 million from private sources, then yeah, I don't want my company under the scrutiny of the unwashed masses who don't understand my business. . . . That's actually terrifying to me."[7] And if alternative forms of channeling capital continue to prove effective (for example, private equity rather than public markets), then the need for going public also declines.

There are countervailing forces, of course. Securitization requires an investment banking function, and public corporations are not the only ones who issue bonds: States and municipal governments do too. But as alternative platforms for intermediating capital proliferate, we may be seeing Wall Street return to its more traditional functions.

Conclusion

THE DECLINE OF public corporations has led to a weaker social safety net, greater inequality, and lower upward mobility. Corporations were the pillars holding up the American economic system and providing stability and opportunity.

Yet on the other hand, the corporate system has long been described as its own form of feudalism. The decline of the corporate system opens up opportunities for new forms of economic organization that are more local, more democratic, and more environmentally sustainable. In this chapter we have described some of these trends. In the next, we consider some alternative paths for the future.

NOW WHAT?

NOW WHAT?

For most of the 20th century, American corporations served as a foundation for economic stability. Their fitful disappearance over the past generation creates a number of social challenges. This section of the book describes some of the most likely scenarios for the future. One possibility is dystopian, with the economy becoming increasingly polarized among a handful of haves and a vast army of have-nots competing to provide them with personal services through various on-demand apps. Alternatively, we have the raw materials for a revival of localism, enhanced by global connections—a "cosmopolitan locavorism" that builds on the ruins of the old corporate economy. As with the response to the rise of the large corporation at the start of the 20th century, which path we take will depend on politics and social movements.

What lies ahead for individuals? What advice should one give a 20-year-old today? In *The Graduate*, the appropriate one-word advice to someone fresh out of college in 1968 was "plastics." In the 1980s, it was "Wall Street"; in the 1990s, "the Web." Since the dot-com crash of 2000, however, it is difficult to find any guidance that would have looked wise in retrospect (mortgage broker? house flipper/reseller? law school?). Along with the threats of automation and globalization, jobs today face the risk of "Uberization": the change from an ongoing job to a discrete task, paid on a piece rate. From driving a taxi to diagnosing and treating illnesses, the personal services that were supposed to be immune to offshoring are in the process of joining the on-demand economy in which free agents compete to provide services for a fixed fee. Recent history suggests that discrete skills (say, in computer coding) may not provide a safe harbor. Liberal education with regular doses of skills updating may be the best course.

CHAPTER 13

POSSIBLE POSTCORPORATE FUTURES

THE DECLINE OF the major American corporation has left a set of pathologies for American society, from rampant inequality and low mobility to a tangled social safety net. There is little reason to expect that large corporations are coming back, least of all in the form of large-scale employers. Zynga is not going to grow up to be Westinghouse, and Facebook will never employ as many people as AT&T did in 1970.

We are in the midst of a third industrial revolution. Each has had a characteristic technology—the steam engine, the assembly line, the smartphone—and each brought about new forms of combining people into productive organizations. But technology alone did not determine what forms these organizations took. The inequities associated with unfettered markets brought out opposition from social movements. Political struggles tamed markets to serve human needs.

This chapter describes two possible scenarios for the future. The first is ubiquitous Uberization, in which jobs are completely decomposed into tasks that are staffed on demand. This is the pathway to the "precariat," with rampant markets and pervasive economic uncertainty. The second is the revival of communities as the locus of economic activity. We have the raw materials for a revival of localism enhanced by global connections: a "cosmopolitan locavorism" that builds on the components of the old corporate economy to create a more democratic and equitable economy.

Industrial revolutions and social change

THE TRANSITION THE American economy is undergoing is not unprecedented. Some describe it as a third industrial revolution.[1] Each of the two prior industrial revolutions also brought about wrenching social changes, as economics and politics collided over how to organize people and productive technology. The original industrial revolution occurred in the decades around the turn of the 19th century. The development of the steam engine to power industrial and transportation equipment combined with the evolution of manufacturing machines (e.g., for spinning and weaving cotton) to permanently transform how goods were produced. Radical increases in productivity led to unprecedented economic growth. At the same time, industrialization and urbanization created massive social dislocation. Cities like Manchester, the center of the British textile industry, were filthy, dangerous, and disease-ridden. The largely unregulated expansion of industry led to the widespread use of child labor, inhumanly long hours, and dangerous working conditions at the bottom, while producing vast fortunes at the top. The "dark Satanic mills" ultimately called forth efforts to tame them, including the birth of labor unions, child labor laws, and the earliest forms of a social safety net.

The second industrial revolution, around the turn of the 20th century, included the development of mass production and mass distribution. Lower cost steel, railroads, and the development of electric power generation in the second half of the 1800s laid the foundation for an explosion of new industries and methods of production, such as the automotive assembly line. Mass production was not just a way of organizing machines. Peter Drucker wrote in 1949:

> Nothing ever before recorded in the history of man equals in speed, universality, and impact the transformation that modern industrial organization has wrought in the foundations of society in the forty years since Henry Ford developed the mass production principle to turn out the Model T. . . . Today it has become abundantly clear that the mass-production principle

is not confined to manufacturing but is *a general principle of human organization for joint work.*[2]

As we have seen, this technology was often most efficiently housed in a corporation. In its early period, mass production technology again produced fortunes at the top and immiseration at the bottom. Chapter 3 described how the Progressive movement worked to tame the modern corporation and to harness its productivity for collective benefit, although it took decades, the Great Depression, war, and a powerful labor movement to reach the accord represented by the Treaty of Detroit.

Our third industrial revolution has been enabled by new kinds of infrastructure, in particular computers, the Internet, and mobile telephony. If the steam engine was the representative innovation of the first industrial revolution, and the Model T exemplified the second, then the smartphone is the avatar of our own age. And if Manchester was the epicenter in 1816, and Detroit in 1916, then Silicon Valley is our epicenter today—even though many of our current innovations are effectively placeless. Drucker noted that mass production was "a general principle of human organization for joint work." We are seeing the birth of something similar today, as ICTs increase the ability to coordinate the efforts of people dispersed around the globe, for little cost. Open-source efforts like Linux and Wikipedia may be as significant an innovation in collaboration as mass production. And the smartphone enables collaboration not just online but on the ground.

As with the prior revolutions, new technologies are producing social dislocation, starting with the collapse of the traditional corporation but extending well beyond it. What is an employee? What does a company owe its community? Does "community" make sense as a construct with today's dispersed forms of enterprise? Will companies even survive?

In each industrial revolution, it was not just technology or "the market" that shaped the future, but political struggles that reined in these new forces. Labor organizations arose in the first industrial revolution; Progressivism and industrial unions arose in response to corporate mass production. In this book I've argued that the corporation as we have known it is no longer the most cost-effective default form of enterprise. New forms create new challenges, and it makes little sense to assume that what worked in 1910, or 1935, will be the best political response today. This chapter considers some possible scenarios for the future. Efforts at predicting the future in times of technological and social change often turn out badly. In early 2000 AOL and Yahoo ruled the Web, Enron was America's most innovative company, the patent on Google's search algorithm had not been issued, and Microsoft was an unstoppable monopoly. Things change. But we can at least hazard some possibilities.

Raw materials

THERE IS A famous scene in the movie *Apollo 13* showing resourcefulness and invention in the face of extreme constraints. Three astronauts are in a capsule designed for two, and carbon dioxide is building up in their atmosphere to potentially toxic levels. The support team back on the ground needs to improvise a solution to save the crew's lives, but of course the team can only use the materials available to the crew within the capsule. The "ingredients" are dumped on a conference table, and the team gets to work coming up with a functioning carbon dioxide scrubber and a set of instructions to construct it, using lithium hydroxide canisters, hoses from space suits, two bags, two socks, the cover of their flight manual, a bungee cord, and duct tape. The hack works, the crew is saved, and we now have the perfect metaphor for creating new institutions from available materials.

What are the relevant raw materials for institutions after the corporation? First, open-source software tools are free and abundant, from server hosting to phone operating systems to creating apps for collective action. Almost anyone can acquire basic coding skills from free online courses.[3] And we have well-developed models for large-scale collaboration on software and content.

Second, capital equipment, from routers to 3-D printers, keeps getting more capable and cheaper. The near-universal fabrication facility will be here in the not-too-distant future, and it will cost much less than we expect. On-demand local production of customized designs will be plausible quite soon. Just as every village had a blacksmith shop, every neighborhood may have a fab facility.[4]

Third, smartphones quickly transitioned from a novelty in 2007 to the most indispensable product in the world for large swathes of the population today. Many Americans are never more than 5 feet from their phone unless they are at the gym or in the pool, always on and always connected.

Fourth, those under age 30 were raised as digital natives and most are entirely comfortable with online technology. They grew up believing that all the world's knowledge is available instantaneously via their phone. For those of us who make a living trying to teach digital natives, this can be a challenge. (Ask a classroom full of undergrads "How many presidents have been left-handed?" or "What is the formula for kurtosis?" or "Where did twerking originate?" and you will quickly learn humility.) But many have a sensibility that problems have solutions, from small ("What's the best way to get to Tiger Stadium from here by bicycle?") to *grande* ("Our house is snowed in and my wife is in labor. How do I deliver a baby?"). And if they have their own solution, they will often make it available to everyone online. (For help with that last problem, visit http://www.wikihow.com/Deliver-a-Baby.)

Finally, we face catastrophic climate change, which demands a global reduction in carbon output, particularly in rich countries. But renewable energy, and solar in particular, have reached a point where they will be cost competitive. Solar power, unlike coal or nuclear, is often most efficiently generated locally. This suggests that power grids in the future might best be organized on a municipal or neighborhood level. We next consider some alternative ways these raw materials might be combined to create either a dystopian or a utopian(ish) future.

A dystopian alternative: ubiquitous Uberization

IN JUST OVER 5 years, Uber grew from a crazy idea that you might have come up with in your dorm room ("What if you could hail a cab from your phone, using its GPS, and you could pay through your phone, and a map would show where the driver was, and you could see their picture, and their ratings from prior customers, and the drivers could rate you back . . . ") to a global business operating in 30 countries with hundreds of thousands of drivers and millions of customers. As Chapter 12 discussed, there are now Ubers for everything. The online platform is an innovation like the assembly line that is not so much a radical technological breakthrough (like the steam engine or the transistor) but a way of organizing existing technology to enable new forms of working together.

The most important thing about Uber is not what it is doing to the taxi industry (although that is surely important, as striking cab drivers vividly demonstrated when they shut down Paris in June 2015). The most important thing is what Uber and other platforms mean for labor markets and how employment is organized. These platforms create a market for buyers and sellers (in this case, of rides) to connect and strike a deal in real time. Drivers do not earn an hourly wage, but compensation for completing a task. Contractors could instead be hired for, say, 4 hours of "whatever I ask you that is legal." Such labor markets already exist in the parking lots of Home Depots across America in the early morning hours, where people who need a work crew for the day (for yard work or crop harvesting or light construction) recruit laborers for a negotiated rate. Economists call this a spot market for labor.

Platforms like Uber make it easy to create a spot market for all kinds of labor. Nobel Prize-winner Ronald Coase wrote in 1937 that "the main reasons why it is profitable to establish a firm would seem to be that there is a cost of using the price mechanism. The most obvious cost of 'organizing' production through the price mechanism is that of discovering what the relevant prices are."[5] Platforms make it cheap to discover prices for labor and other inputs. They reduce the transaction costs of using the market, and make alternatives to the firm more economical. They create the virtual version of the Home Depot parking lot at dawn, but for tasks far beyond yard work.

Suppose that there was an app like Uber in which prospective workers published profiles showing their certifications for particular skills (yard work; Python coding; kidney transplants), and ratings or endorsements by prior "users." Someone needing a work crew for the day could post a virtual sign-up sheet, and potential contractors with the relevant skills could bid against each other to be in the first, say, five slots. Those who "won" would find their own way to the worksite. Now consider all low-skill, manual-labor jobs in America that cannot be offshored, all staffed on a daily basis through a competitive bidding process. (These are the jobs at the low end of our bipolar labor markets.) Many of these jobs could be instantly transformed into tasks; employees would become contractors. And it will not stop with low-skill tasks. We normally think of physicians as being at the other end of the labor market, but there are already apps for virtual doctor visits that allow consumers to describe their symptoms (using their phone or tablet's camera if appropriate), converse with an actual physician, and get a diagnosis and treatment plan. Need an antibiotic prescription for a urinary tract infection? There's an app for that.[6] Who would have thought that physicians would end up working in call centers on a piece-rate basis?

This vision imagines that workers are more or less interchangeable. It doesn't much matter which physician you see because they all know how to deal with a UTI. But what about corporate culture? If people can easily be swapped out, then why do companies put so much effort into writing heartfelt mission statements, selecting just the right kinds of people, and socializing them into the company's unique and visionary culture? Some companies do that, and some will continue to do so into the future. But the design of work is not a constant: Changes in technology create innovations in how work itself is organized. The mature version of the assembly line was designed to require as little skill and training as possible. The work was unbearably tedious, and turnover was high; jobs were designed so that workers would be easily replaceable. The automated assembly line provided its own form of supervision. This will happen to platform-based work as well.

Major retailers and restaurants today have adopted an electronic version of the assembly line using workforce management systems. Checkout clerks are continuously measured on how quickly they scan each product and complete each transaction, every hour, all day, every day. Sales clerks are tracked based on how much merchandise they sell and whether they are effectively upselling customers, all day every day. The system requires few human managers because somewhere at a corporate operations center, employees are being evaluated and compared by the all-seeing HR staff.[7] In an increasing number of restaurant chains, tablet computers allow restaurant customers to place their orders and pay their bill by credit card; servers are evaluated not just on how much they sold, but how the customers rated them at the end of the meal.[8] The headache of scheduling employees, and hearing their tales of woe about why they need Saturday off for their grandma's funeral, is no longer in the hands of management: it's done by an algorithm.[9] The successors to Frederick Taylor, father of scientific management and the dreaded time-and-motion study, are the designers of workforce management software.

If you were an efficiency-minded IT consultant designing a new concept in retail management, given the tools available today, you might consider being the Uber of retail. Associates (as minimum-wage retail employees are inevitably called) hate being scheduled by algorithms. They hate having to work until closing, open the store the next day, close again, open again, and then have 5 days off when they really, really need the hours to pay their rent. The new rules about health insurance, and what counts as part-time or full-time, are a pain in the neck. But customers have not responded well to self-checkout, making it difficult to do without human labor entirely. Thus, the concept arises of stores staffed entirely by app-based contractors, who will be referred to as "self-employed micro-entrepreneurs." Choose your own hours! Work at different stores, for as many or as few shifts as you like! (Note: Subject to availability.) Take vacations whenever you want! Surge pricing! Enjoy fun gamefied competitions to see who gets to take a shift!

Interfering government bureaucrats may insist that these people are employees. So to provide another layer of potential legal insulation, each contractor will form an LLC and pay a certification fee to be a "franchisee." (Something like this is already going on in the construction and janitorial services industries.[10]) As part of the franchise qualification, they can be trained and certified for different tasks, as in IT. If recent college graduates are willing to work for free as "interns" in order to get a foot in the door, why not take the next step and charge them? Universities have been telling students to be entrepreneurial and control their own destiny. This will answer that call, by providing an on-ramp to being your own boss. The corporation, as an employer, will be replaced by the platform, matching tasks to micro-entrepreneurs.

If you are a 22-year-old libertarian who loves the novels of Ayn Rand, this may strike you as a vision of paradise. Corporations were a kind of socialism in miniature, with jobs and careers being paid not according to their market value that day, but according to some bureaucratic rules about merit and seniority and fairness. Why not introduce market forces to as many human interactions as possible and eliminate the distorting effects of nonmarket institutions like internal labor markets? Escape the corporate plantation! Live free or die! On the other hand, if you are older than 22, and have applied for a mortgage, or had to take time out due to illness or childbirth, or planned for more than one semester into the future, you may see some drawbacks to this world of all markets, all the time.

The ability to secure labor on demand at varying levels of skill is the true significance of Uber. It is the "gray goo scenario" of employment. The gray goo scenario, attributable to Eric Drexler, is the idea of self-replicating nano-robots consuming all life on Earth, leaving its surface a mass of gray goo. The spread of Uberization has the prospect of eliminating much traditional employment in favor of on-demand tasks. In the absence of social and labor reforms, this is perhaps the most plausible future scenario.

A utopian(ish) alternative:
the revival of local economies

TECHNOLOGY IS NOT destiny. The same technologies that can produce a gray goo scenario can also help create a very different future. As with prior industrial revolutions, however, this will require politics and social movements. Uninhibited market forces will lead us toward the digital dark Satanic mills. There are already some signs of this on Amazon's Mechanical Turk, where competition for online human intelligence tasks (HITs) is fierce, global, and relentless. It is not uncommon for Turkers to earn well under minimum wage competing for tasks compensated by pennies.[11] Uberization promises more of this kind of dynamic, as more and more tasks become subject to competition. Life is tough trapped in a situation with precarious income and no path forward.

It doesn't have to be this way. Regulators and courts still have some control over how employment is defined. Digital immiseration is not inevitable. But a better future will require social movements and political action. It will also require rethinking some of our economic institutions to serve as alternatives to the corporation. Corporations did not just provide goods and services, or shareholder value: They provided jobs, benefits, and economic security for the people who worked for them. Those needs will have to be met somehow, and markets alone will not do it.

It is worth reminding ourselves that business is a means, not an end in itself. We do business and create corporations to achieve something else, just as we might own a truck to be able to transport things. People can become considerably attached to their trucks, or emotionally invested in their corporations, but we are better served by regarding them as means, and focusing on the ends. What needs are served? If corporations can no longer provide long-term economic security, what kinds of alternative institutional arrangements could? What can replace the corporation to make us better off, not worse off? And where can these arrangements be "housed"?

In 1987, Daniel Bell noted that as the international economy was becoming more integrated, nation-states were fragmenting. His diagnosis was that "the nation-state is becoming too small for the big problems of life, and too big for the small problems of life."[12] His insight has become more true with time. Climate change is a planetary problem that individual states seem too paralyzed to address. Pandemics skip across borders. National taxation systems benefit those wily enough to stash their loot in offshore havens. International terrorist groups operate seamlessly across borders. National boundaries do not encompass our global problems. Yet national governments are not the right level to address local safety, access to child care, or the potholes in our streets. Partly as a result of this tension, we see failed nation-states, para-states (for example, ISIS), breakaway movements (Scotland, Catalonia, Quebec, Kurdistan, Texas), tensions within supranational federations (for example, between Greece and the EU), and a surprising enthusiasm for mayors.[13]

Environmentalist Bill McKibben suggested that the size and location of the institution should match the size of the project.[14] In some sense we may be observing adjustments in this direction, as municipal or regional authorities seem like about the right scale for many of our collective problems. Notably, vesting power at the community level appeals to both the left and the right. The left fears distant giant corporations. The right loathes centralized government. Both see the appeal of local control.

The pivot toward the community—rather than the nation-state or the corporation—also accords well with some of the technological developments we have discussed. Technologies increasingly favor distributed manufacturing, as facilities for low-cost CNC equipment and 3-D printing can be established at the city or neighborhood level. Local coffee roasters and breweries have flourished in the past two decades. Why buy flat-pack furniture shipped from China if it could be cut on demand, from materials you chose, in your own neighborhood? Moreover, since open-source designs are freely available on the Web, furniture and other goods can be easily customized for one-off production. Or why buy new at all if online neighborhood market-places allow swapping or bartering? Sites like Nextdoor.com demonstrate that highly localized social networks can be especially valuable. Why buy a cheap lawnmower or belt sander when the neighborhood could cooperatively own high-quality tools to be shared with the tool-share app? Professor Jessica Gordon Nembhard shows that generations of African American communities pioneered a number of sophisticated institutions and social practices for sharing, even without the benefit of smartphone apps.[15] The sorts of "sharing" apps that are enabling Zipcar, Airbnb, and other online marketplaces could be used for a wide array of nonmarket forms of sharing.

Infrastructure may also favor the local. Neighborhood solar power grids have much to recommend them, and mesh networks at the neighborhood level may be a viable alternative means of providing Internet access. Locally oriented economic institutions were largely supplanted with the rise of the corporation, but we can reconstitute them.

Larger-scale organizations can also be transformed by ICTs. In contrast to the all-contractor organization described in the previous section, how about a collectively owned and managed business, where the profit stays with those who do the work? Instead of designing technologies to render labor as anonymous and interchangeable as possible, we could have technologies that enable democratic participation in decision making and draw on the insights of those doing the work to make decisions.[16] Not all decisions require a town hall meeting; many could be made with a quick check-in on a smartphone ("rank order these five choices"). Where is the workplace democracy app that will turn General Motors into a kibbutz?

Perhaps one reason we have not seen more "community platforms" is the dominance of the venture capital/IPO model of startup development, which favors business models that can scale quickly for sale. On the other hand, the early days of software were also dominated by for-profit providers, and only later did open source achieve its position of prominence.

One concern about community-level organization is that it can be parochial. This is not, however, a plea to return to village life. Much of the world's cultural output has been online for years; music, literature, film, recipes, whatever can be digitized. Moreover, we have already seen that the separation of design from manufacture, and the coming proliferation of universal fab facilities, mean that the world's designs can be produced anywhere. It seems likely that we will see the flourishing of a "cosmopolitan locavorism" that combines the best of world and local culture and engages in global exchanges of ideas and designs.

Conclusion

NEW TECHNOLOGIES CAN render old ways of organizing obsolete and make new ways possible. As with prior industrial revolutions, our current transition is creating great uncertainty while opening up new possibilities. Left undisturbed, our current trajectory points toward Uberization, in which market forces reach deep into organizations and turn daily interactions into market transactions. But with suitable modification, nudged by political movements, we could instead see a revival of local economies, enriched by local production and access to global designs. Local and democratic forms of organization could address the needs formerly met by the corporation.

In the final chapter, we consider what individuals can do to best prepare themselves for the challenges ahead.

CHAPTER 14

NAVIGATING A POSTCORPORATE ECONOMY

I**F YOU HAVE** made it this far in the book, you will realize that these are turbulent times and that the potential futures I foresee range from the utopian to the nightmarish. In the face of these very different possibilities, I give a brief rundown of our current situation when it comes to jobs and suggest some "all-weather" guidance that features liberal education with a dose of technology skills.

Our current situation

IF YOU WANT to make your way in this new world, it helps to have a map of how it works. I hope this book has helped provide a sketch of such a map. We are on much surer ground when describing the old world that is falling apart than the new one that will take its place, but there is an emerging outline for some broad guidance.

At his college graduation party, Benjamin Braddock in *The Graduate* gets some helpful advice about his future from a businessman. "I want to say one word to you. Just one word. Are you listening? Plastics." That word might have been great advice in 1968. What would today's equivalent be? Solar? 3-D printing? Biodegradable plastics? Even the idea of a promising industry does not align with the emerging shape of our economy. Is Uber a software company, a transportation company, a marketplace, or something else?

The quest for a good bet or a safe path is misplaced, given the capriciousness of the forces at work. Electronics would have seemed like a great choice in 1999. Five years later the industry had been largely offshored, shedding hundreds of thousands of jobs in the United States. Accounting was the most stable of careers—some might even say boring—until Arthur Andersen went bankrupt in 2001 after the Enron collapse. Law school was always a safe Plan B for those willing to invest in a few more years of school. But new enrollments in 2014 were down 30% compared to 2010, as much of the work of junior associates can now be done offshore or by software.[1]

Our current economy is like a Powerball lottery, in which a handful of job seekers achieve massive wealth overnight, while others face pervasive insecurity.[2] Teen programmers sell their app to Facebook and retire before reaching drinking age, while competitors with essentially identical products lose out. Lucky homeowners in Florida cash in before the bubble bursts, while others are left underwater (financially if not yet actually). Random Korean pop stars hit an unexpected cultural cord and go viral, while thousands of others go unseen.

In recent years, the standard advice to avoid having your job automated or offshored has been to find work in a field that requires the in-person delivery of services.[3] Surgeon, personal trainer, massage therapist, manicurist: Any personal service that caters disproportionately to the well-off is presumably unlikely to be replaced by a robot or an outsourcing firm in India. But the new threat to these jobs is Uberization—that is, they may devolve from more-or-less steady jobs to on-demand tasks, subject to ongoing competition. Customers may prefer the personal touch of a particular massage therapist or primary care physician, but if every massage is an opportunity to go out to the market and save a few dollars, then . . . . Thus, the new calculus around jobs is not just "is it valuable?" and "can it be automated or offshored?" but "will it be Uberized so I end up having to hustle all day every day?"

Pervasive uncertainty is the hallmark of major economic transitions. This time, the uncertainty runs unusually deep. Basic categories we use to understand the economy, like "industry" or "employee," no longer mean what they used to. For example, how many people are unemployed—that is, they want a full-time job but do not have one? Published unemployment figures have gone down sharply since the depth of the Great Recession. At the same time, the rate of labor-force participation has dropped to its lowest point since 1977, when far fewer women were in the paid workforce (see Figure 14.1). The decline is partly due to people living longer and baby boomers beginning to retire. But there are other factors at work as well. An unknown number are stopping out of the labor force entirely, for a variety of reasons. Social Security Disability Insurance has come to function as a kind of stealth unemployment program. The number of people receiving SSDI, who are not counted on the unemployment rolls, has increased continuously over the past two decades and now substantially outnumbers the formally unemployed (see Figure 14.2). Few ever leave the SSDI rolls: They are, in a sense, permanently unemployed.[4] And the number of those making a living in the temp economy is also hard to track with current data. We don't really know how many people are living off a combination of part-time jobs or Uber-like tasks (a class Robert Kuttner labeled "the Task Rabbit economy"[5]). In short, our current job market is like an unmapped island full of dense rain forests, prone to earthquakes that rearrange the landscape, and with a volcano at the center. Welcome!

FIGURE 14.1 Civilian labor-force participation (percentage), 1980–2015

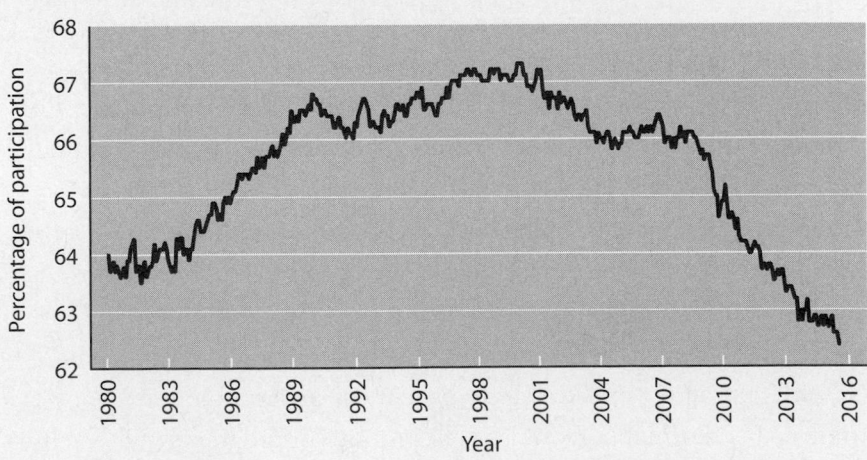

Source: Bureau of Labor Statistics

FIGURE 14.2 Number of people receiving Social Security Disability Insurance in thousands, 1995–2015

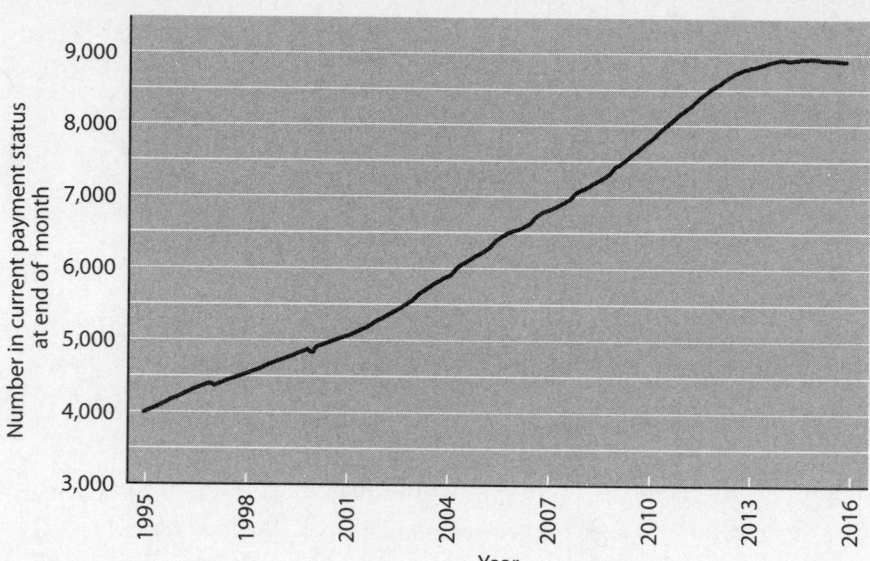

Source: Social Security Administration

The enduring appeal of liberal education

I HAVE TO declare a conflict of interest: I teach at a university, and I am a true believer in the intrinsic value of education. It is therefore distressing to see those who should know better describing education as if its sole purpose were training for a job. Washington even considered publishing ratings that evaluated colleges as a financial investment, comparing the projected value of future wages with the cost of attending the school.[6] Colleges would receive the sort of ratings that Morningstar gives to mutual funds. Some politicians have been even more dismissive. In describing his budget priorities, Florida's Governor Rick Scott said, "If I'm going to take money from a citizen to put into education, then I'm going to take that money to create jobs. So I want that money to go to degrees where people can get jobs in this state. Is it a vital interest of the state to have more anthropologists? I don't think so."[7] Presumably Florida's college football programs will be eliminated on the same basis, as few of its players go on to paid careers as professional football players in the state of Florida. (At the moment fewer than 20 players on the state's three professional football teams attended Florida's public universities.) Or maybe Florida's anthropology majors can redeem themselves by becoming Uber drivers in Miami?

The point of education is not (just) to get a job, or to get a credential, but to be prepared for life. Focusing exclusively on a job at the end of college is likely to be self-defeating, particularly during a time of rapid technological change. Indeed, Governor Scott seemed to imply that the Florida State government is well qualified to predict where the jobs will be 5 to 10 years out. Ten years ago there were no smartphones, no iPad, and thus no industry for mobile apps. Platform businesses like Uber and the rest of the on-demand economy would have been inconceivable. On the other hand, in 2006 a sizeable chunk of Florida's economy was made of up real estate and related industries: mortgage brokers and originators, real estate agents, marble countertop installers, house flippers/resellers. Since house prices surely never go down (and climate change will have no influence on the state's shoreline), the safest bet for long-term employment in the Sunshine State would have been real estate.

It is extremely risky business trying to predict which firms or jobs or industries will be winners in a few years' time. Energy, finance, and telecommunications seem like great bets—unless you mean Enron, Lehman Brothers, and BlackBerry. Scan the covers of business magazines from 10 years ago and you will appreciate just how rare it is to get this right. The world moves fast, but education should prepare you for the long run.

Preparation for a life of learning and citizenship is the traditional mission of the liberal arts. Studying philosophy teaches us to think logically and argue persuasively. Art helps us understand how materials come together to create their effects. Anthropology gives us an understanding of human culture, how it is expressed, how it evolves—which can be especially useful in strange and exotic Florida. Liberal education has an enduring value beyond the specific subjects studied, which is why it has survived longer than, say, stenography or e-commerce majors.

On the other hand, it is also essential to have tangible skills. Al Capone is quoted as saying, "You can get much farther with a kind word and a gun than you can with a kind word alone." I would update this: You can get much farther with a liberal arts education and coding skills than you can with a liberal arts education alone. Understanding how the Web works is indispensable today, even if you have no particular desire to code your own website. Enterprises increasingly operate like a Web page, drawing on dispersed resources to create a performance. (If you have not yet right-clicked on your favorite website to see the underlying code that produces it, you should.)

It is not difficult to learn to code, particularly if you have a logical turn of mind (perhaps thanks to that philosophy training). At the University of Michigan, we run a weeklong Big Data Summer Camp that trains complete neophytes in Python, SQL, and how to use APIs. (If none of these terms rings a bell, you might want to consider getting some training yourself.) A week is enough to get some basic skills; a month of practice is enough to equip you for a dissertation. The goal is not to become a professional programmer, but to have at least a passing understanding of some of the key technologies of our time and to be more useful at whatever job you are in. And if you do want to qualify for a specific job, an 8- or 12-week course at the computer science school General Assembly or other similar providers may be a reasonable choice. Learning a specific programming language will not provide you with a lifetime of employment, as COBOL veterans can testify: Languages and platforms change. But learning to think like a programmer is an extremely valuable addition to liberal education and transfers well.

What is perhaps most surprising is that these skills are still scarce, and therefore still valuable. I routinely (and annoyingly) ask audiences at my talks "who can tell me what API stands for?" and it is rare that more than one or two hands go up (it means "application programming interface," and it defines how programs or websites can access data, such as links to appropriate Google Maps). Most of those over 30 really have very little idea how the online world works, which is to the advantage of the digital natives. Remember, if an angry bear is chasing you and a companion, you don't need to outrun the bear—just the companion. And you don't need a PhD in computer science to have enough skills to be valuable.

Careers in a Powerball job market

NO ONE GREW up wishing to be an Uber driver or a Turker on MTurk. Most would consider these to be gigs on the way to a broader career ambition. How should we think about careers differently?

Perhaps the most frequently given piece of advice is to follow your passion. This is terrible advice for any number of reasons. Some follow their passions by pursuing a career that their 12-year-old self wanted. It is fair to assume that any career that appeals to a young person is either inaccessible (basketball player, ballerina, president) or too crowded (veterinarian), or both (musician). Others follow a passion for a specific domain, like "travel" or "chocolate," where it is difficult or impossible to make a living.

Do not follow your passion. That's for narcissists. Be of service and passion will follow. What the world needs today is passionate people who actually know how to do something—say, liberal arts graduates who know what an API is. Identify genuine human needs and find a way to serve them, and you will make your living. There is no shortage of needs to be addressed, as we have seen in prior chapters. Being able to identify these needs can take some empathy and background. Meanwhile, the app economy is largely populated with products that were obviously created by "bro-grammers" who stinted on the liberal arts education. An app for hookups! An app for cocktails! An app for pizza!

The utopian vision in the prior chapter can be realized by institution-builders who understand the current socioeconomic transition. For example, one of the hazards of the precariat workforce is volatile income from week to week. Some weeks a worker gets many hours and earns a big paycheck, other weeks less so. A stable income is essential for planning, paying bills, and saving for the future. The app Even.me provides an income-smoothing service for a $3 weekly fee. It calculates your average weekly income based on the past few months' pay, then during weeks when you make more, it deposits your income in an insured account at a partner bank; when you make less, it provides an interest-free loan to top you up. Although it is a for-profit business, it serves a critical need in an innovative way.[8] It is easy to imagine similar businesses that match, say, excess food inventory at stores or farms to those who need food, elders with time to spare with kids who need child care or tutoring, and so on. Someone needs to be designing and installing those neighborhood solar power grids; creating resilient mesh networks to provide Internet access to low-income communities; customizing open-source designs for furniture to be produced using locally available materials; or designing that workplace democracy app to enable collaborative decision making. The cost of creating an enterprise can be quite low these days, as many of the parts are available free or cheap. Failure is common, but today the investment is small, so the risk is not catastrophic.

Technology blogger Peter Reinhardt distinguishes between jobs that are "above the API" (those who are building the apps and the computer systems) and those that are "below the API" (the worker bees who deliver the actual services: drivers at Uber, pickers at Amazon warehouses, waitresses at Chili's). There is no career path from Uber driver to coder, and the jobs below the API are the ones destined for automation.[9] It is clear that the best bet is to be above the API. Or, as accidental drug kingpin Walter White put it in *Breaking Bad* when he describes why he is not afraid of threatening people knocking on his door: "I am the one who knocks." Those above the API are the ones who knock.

Conclusion

THESE ARE SURELY uncertain times for those who have to make a living. Jobs are volatile, and it is impossible to give surefire advice about careers in this new world, where the meaning of basic categories like "industry" and "employee" are changing. Liberal education coupled with tangible skills in coding are likely to be the best preparation. Understand our transition. Be of service.

RESOURCES

Throughout this book, I rely on information that is readily available online. As with any work based on research, it is certain that others would draw different conclusions from the data I use. To make it easier to verify or criticize, interested readers, especially journalists and researchers, will find the following resources particularly helpful.

Bureau of Labor Statistics. The BLS is the authoritative source on employment statistics in the US, including historical information about employment within each industry: http://www.bls.gov/data/.

Securities and Exchange Commision. The SEC's EDGAR contains securities filings for corporations listed on US stock markets, starting for most in 1994. The 10-K (annual report) contains financial and employment information. The DEF 14A (proxy statement) includes information about corporate officers and directors as well as corporate ownership. The S-1 (IPO prospectus) describes how voting rights are allocated, among other things. Filings by particular companies are available at http://www.sec.gov/edgar/searchedgar/companysearch.html.

Wharton Research Data Services. More comprehensive annual financial and accounting information on US corporations, often going back to 1950, is available at the WRDS (for a fee) at https://wrds-web .wharton.upenn.edu/wrds/.

Mergent. Prior to online data sources, *Moody's Industrial Manuals* provided compilations of corporate financial and management information beginning in roughly 1900. Many of these old sources are archived in accessible form at http://www.mergentonline.com/login.php.

Initial public offerings. The best source of data on IPOs in the United States is provided by Professor Jay Ritter at the Warrington College of Business, University of Florida: https://site.warrington.ufl .edu/ritter/ipo-data/.

World Bank. The World Bank compiles hundreds of economic and social variables annually for every country, often as far back as 1960, in its *World Development Indicators* database: http://data.worldbank.org/data-catalog/world-development-indicators.

United Nations Development Programme. The UNDP's Human Development Reports data complement the World Bank data in providing more detailed indicators of human well-being around the world: http://hdr.undp.org/en/data.

Income inequality. Three sources of cross-national data on inequality for extended time periods are the Standardized World Income Inequality Database at the University of Iowa (http://myweb.uiowa.edu/fsolt/swiid/swiid.html), the United Nations World Income Inequality Database (https://www.wider.unu.edu/project/wiid-world-income-inequality-database), and the Luxembourg Income Study Database (http://www.lisdatacenter.org/).

NOTES

CHAPTER 1 CORPORATIONS IN AMERICA AND AROUND THE WORLD

1. For summary statistics on the significance of public corporations to the American economy, see Gerald F. Davis (2013), "After the corporation," *Politics & Society* 41(2): 283–308.

2. Gerald F. Davis (2008), "A new finance capitalism? Mutual funds and ownership re-concentration in the United States," *European Management Review* 5: 11–21.

3. "Mitt Romney Says 'Corporations Are People,'" Philip Rucker, *Washington Post*, August 11, 2011, http://www.washingtonpost.com /politics/mitt-romney-says-corporations-are-people/2011/08/11 /gIQABwZ38I_story.html.

4. The text of the Supreme Court decision is available at https://www.law .cornell.edu/supremecourt/text/17/518.

5. See more about Royal Caribbean's annual report and the tax benefits of Liberian incorporation at http://www.sec.gov/Archives/edgar /data/884887/000088488715000025/rcl-20141231x10k.htm.

6. An excellent introduction to LLCs and other alternatives to incorporation is Larry E. Ribstein (2009), *The Rise of the Uncorporation* (Oxford: Oxford University Press).

7. "McDonald's to Raise Pay at Outlets It Operates," Stephanie Strom, *New York Times*, April 1, 2015, http://www.nytimes.com/2015/04/02 /business/mcdonalds-raising-pay-for-employees.html?_r=0.

8. See Forbes profile in "America's Largest Private Companies 2014" at http://www.forbes.com/companies/koch-industries/.

9. "Dell's Life after Wall Street," Quentin Hardy, *New York Times*, November 2, 2014, http://www.nytimes.com/2014/11/03/business /dells-life-after-wall-street.html.

10. See the General Motors website for full descriptions of the board at http://www.gm.com/company/aboutGM/board_of_directors0.html.

11. See Toyota's most recent annual report at http://www.toyota-global .com/investors/ir_library/annual/pdf/2014/p34_43.pdf.

12. Laws governing Daimler's board are described at http://www.daimler.com/dai/supervisoryboard.

13. Geely's board is listed at http://www.geelyauto.com.hk/en/management.html.

14. Klaus Weber, Gerald F. Davis, and Michael Lounsbury (2009), "Policy as myth and ceremony? The global spread of stock exchanges, 1980–2005," *Academy of Management Journal* 52: 1319–47.

15. Figures on stock markets available from the World Bank's *World Development Indicators* at http://databank.worldbank.org/data/reports.aspx?source=world-development-indicators.

16. Peter Hall and David Soskice (2001), *Varieties of Capitalism: The Institutional Foundations of Comparative Advantage* (Oxford: Oxford University Press); and Bruno Amable (2003), *The Diversity of Modern Capitalism* (Oxford: Oxford University Press).

17. Gerald F. Davis (2009), *Managed by the Markets: How Finance Reshaped America* (Oxford: Oxford University Press).

18. US Steel's 1910 assets estimated at $1.37 billion by *Moody's Industrial Manual*. See US federal government total revenues at $874.8 million at http://www.usgovernmentrevenue.com/year_revenue_1910USbn_16bs1n.

19. Adolph A. Berle and Gardiner C. Means (1932), *The Modern Corporation and Private Property* (Modern Reprint: 1991 edition; New Brunswick, NJ: Transaction).

20. "GM's 'Engine Charlie' Wilson Learned to Live with a Misquote," Justin Hyde, *Detroit Free Press*, September 14, 2008, http://archive.freep.com/article/20080914/BUSINESS01/809140308/GM-s-Engine-Charlie-Wilson-learned-live-misquote.

21. Employment data by industry accessed from the Bureau of Labor Statistics at http://www.bls.gov/data/#employment.

22. Figures on listed companies from the World Bank's *World Development Indicators* at http://databank.worldbank.org/data/reports.aspx?source=world-development-indicators.

23. Employment figures from annual 10-K statements accessed at the US Securities and Exchange Commission's EDGAR at http://www.sec.gov/edgar/searchedgar/companysearch.html. For Netflix: http://www.sec.gov/Archives/edgar/data/1065280/000106528015000006/nflx201410k.htm. For Blockbuster: http://www.sec.gov/Archives/edgar/data/1085734/000119312505063510/d10k.htm.

CHAPTER 2 HOW THE CORPORATION CONQUERED AMERICA

1. For a history of the corporate explosion around the turn of the 20th century, see William G. Roy (1997), *Socializing Capital: The Rise of the Large Industrial Corporation in America* (Princeton: Princeton University Press).

2. "Dow Jones Industrial Average Historical Components," accessed from S&P Dow Jones Indices at http://www.djindexes.com/mdsidx /downloads/brochure_info/Dow_Jones_Industrial_Average_Historical _Components.pdf.

3. Ibid.

4. Alfred D. Chandler (1977), *The Visible Hand: The Managerial Revolution in American Business* (Cambridge, MA: Belknap Press).

5. Mark J. Roe (1994), *Strong Managers, Weak Owners: The Political Roots of American Corporate Finance* (Princeton: Princeton University Press).

6. "'The Rouge: Yesterday, Today, and Tomorrow,'" Lindsay-Jean Hard, *Urban and Regional Planning Economic Development Handbook*, The University of Michigan Taubman, College of Architecture and Urban Planning, December 4, 2005, http://www.umich.edu/~econdev /riverrouge/.

7. Ford's 2015 proxy statement explains the voting rights of its Class B shares, controlled by a Ford family trust: http://www.sec.gov/Archives /edgar/data/37996/000104746915002836/a2223357zdef14a.htm#QA5.

8. See Roy, *Socializing Capital*, for the financial aspects of the merger wave at the turn of the 20th century.

9. Gerald F. Davis (2015), "Corporate Power in the 21st Century," in ed. Subramanian Rangan, *Performance and Progress: Essays on Capitalism, Business and Society* (Oxford: Oxford University Press).

10. Berle and Means, *Modern Corporation*, 46, 356 (see chap. 1, n. 19).

11. Virginia Woolf (1924), *Mr. Bennett and Mrs. Brown* (London: Hogarth Press), 4.

12. David Harvey (1990), *The Condition of Postmodernity: An Enquiry into the Origins of Cultural Change* (Cambridge: Blackwell).

13. Peter Drucker (September 1949), "The new society I: Revolution by mass production," *Harper's Magazine*, 21–30.

CHAPTER 3 TAMING THE CORPORATION

1. John Steinbeck (1939), *The Grapes of Wrath*, (New York: Penguin), 38–39.

2. "President Jackson's Veto Message Regarding the Bank of the United States; July 10, 1832," accessed at Yale Law School's Avalon Project, http://avalon.law.yale.edu/19th_century/ajveto01.asp.

3. Gerald F. Davis and Mark S. Mizruchi (1999), "The money center cannot hold: Commercial banks in the U.S. system of corporate governance," *Administrative Science Quarterly* 44: 215–39. For a history of fragmentation in American banking, see Mark J. Roe, *Strong Managers, Weak Owners*.

4. Louis D. Brandeis (1914), *Other People's Money: And How the Bankers Use It* (New York: Frederick A. Stokes Company).

5. J. Bradford DeLong (1991), "Did JP Morgan's Men Add Value? An Economist's Perspective on Financial Capitalism," in ed. P. Temin, *Inside the Business Enterprise: Historical Perspectives on the Use of Information* (Chicago: University of Chicago), 205–36.

6. For an excellent history of the spread of share ownership in the United States before 1930, see Julia C. Ott (2011), *When Wall Street Met Main Street: The Quest for an Investors' Democracy* (Cambridge MA: Harvard University Press).

7. For a history of merger movements in the US and their effect on corporate form, see Neil Fligstein (1990), *The Transformation of Corporate Control* (Cambridge MA: Harvard University Press).

8. The text of Roosevelt's New Nationalism speech is widely available online, including at the White House website: https://www.whitehouse .gov/blog/2011/12/06/archives-president-teddy-roosevelts-new -nationalism-speech.

CHAPTER 4 THE POSTWAR ERA OF CORPORATE DOMINANCE

1. See Chapter 1, Figure 1.1 for GM's employment figures.

2. James N. Baron, Frank R. Dobbin, and P. Devereaux Jennings (1986), "War and peace: The evolution of modern personnel administration in U.S. Industry," *American Journal of Sociology* 92: 350–83.

3. On the Treaty of Detroit, see Frank Levy and Peter Temin (2007), *Inequality and Institutions in 20th Century America* (Massachusetts Institute of Technology Department of Economics); and J. Adam Cobb (2012), *From the 'Treaty of Detroit' to the 401(k): The Development and Evolution of Privatized Retirement in the United States* (unpublished dissertation, University of Michigan).

4. Gerald F. Davis and J. Adam Cobb (2010), "Corporations and economic inequality around the world: The paradox of hierarchy," *Research in Organizational Behavior* 30: 35–53.

5. Ibid., for more on ITT and the organizational forces shaping income inequality.

6. "Systemic Task Force Report to the Chair of the Equal Employment Opportunity Commission," March 2006, Appendix C, http://www.eeoc .gov/eeoc/task_reports/systemic.cfm.

7. Nixon's "Statement on Signing the Tax Reform Act of 1969" is available from The American Presidency Project at the University of California, Santa Barbara, http://www.presidency.ucsb.edu/ws/?pid=2388.

8. Dean LeBaron and Lawrence S. Speidell (1987), "Why Are the Parts Worth More Than the Sum? 'Chop Shop,' a Corporate Valuation Model," in eds. L. E. Brown and E. S. Rosengren, *The Merger Boom* (Boston: Federal Reserve Bank of Boston).

CHAPTER 5 SHAREHOLDERS GET THE UPPER HAND

1. Gerald F. Davis, Kristina A. Diekmann, and Catherin H. Tinsley (1994), "The decline and fall of the conglomerate firm in the 1980s: The deinstitutionalization of an organizational form," *American Sociological Review* 59: 547–70.

2. Harold Geneen (1997), *The Synergy Myth: And Other Ailments of Business Today* (New York: St. Martin's).

3. LeBaron and Speidell, "Why Are the Parts Worth More Than the Sum?" 87 (see chap. 4, n. 8).

4. Henry G. Manne (1965), "Mergers and the market for corporate control," *Journal of Political Economy* 73: 110–20.

5. For a brief history of how considerations of market power versus efficiency shaped antitrust, see "The Merger Guidelines and the Integration of Efficiencies into Antitrust Review of Horizontal Mergers," by William J. Kolasky and Andrew R. Dick, http://www.justice.gov/atr /hmerger/11254.htm.

6. Gerald F. Davis and Suzanne K. Stout (1992), "Organization theory and the market for corporate control: A dynamic analysis of the characteristics of large takeover targets, 1980–1990," *Administrative Science Quarterly* 37: 605–33.

7. Ibid.

8. Bernard S. Black (1992), "The value of institutional investor monitoring: The empirical evidence," *UCLA Law Review* 39: 895–939.

9. Davis, Diekmann, and Tinsley, "The decline and fall of the conglomerate firm in the 1980s," 547–70.

10. Drucker, "The new society I," 21–30 (see chap. 2, n. 13).

11. Carl Kaysen (1957), "The social significance of the modern corporation," *American Economic Review* (Papers and Proceedings) 47(2): 311–19.

12. Gerald F. Davis and Tracy A. Thompson (1994), "A social movement perspective on corporate control," *Administrative Science Quarterly* 39: 141–73.

13. Michael C. Jensen and Kevin J. Murphy (May–June 1990), "CEO incentives—it's not how much you pay, but how," *Harvard Business Review* 68 (3): 138–153.

14. Employee Benefit Research Institute, "FAQs about benefits": http://www.ebri.org/publications/benfaq/index.cfm?fa=retfaq14.

15. Davis, "A new finance capitalism?" 11–21 (see chap. 1, n. 2).

16. Gerald F. Davis and Natalie Cotton (2007), "Political Consequences of Financial Market Expansion: Does Buying a Mutual Fund Turn You Republican?" presented at the American Sociological Association Annual Meetings, New York; and Natalie C. Cotton Nessler, and Gerald F. Davis (2012), "Stock ownership, political beliefs, and party identification from the 'Ownership Society' to the financial meltdown," *Accounting, Economics, and Law* 2(2).

17. Investment Company Institute, *2015 Investment Company Fact Book: A Review of Trends and Activities in the US Investment Company Industry*, http://www.icifactbook.org/.

18. Figures from Davis, "After the corporation." Data compiled from Bureau Van Dijk's Orbis dataset, http://www.bvdinfo.com/en-gb/our-products/company-information/international-products/orbis.

19. For a discussion of the Clinton Administration's love affair with the financial markets, see Davis *Managed by the Markets*, (chap. 1, n. 17).

20. Davis and Thompson, "A social movement perspective on corporate control."

21. "An investor calls," *The Economist*, February 7, 2015, http://www.economist.com/news/briefing/21642175-sometimes-ill-mannered-speculative-and-wrong-activists-are-rampant-they-will-change-american.

CHAPTER 6 NIKEFICATION AND
THE RISE OF THE VIRTUAL CORPORATION

1. John Byrne, "The virtual corporation," *BusinessWeek*, February 7, 1993, http://www.bloomberg.com/bw/stories/1993-02-07/the-virtual -corporation.

2. Nike's annual reports, with information on revenues and employment, are available at the Securities and Exchange Commission's EDGAR site: http://www.sec.gov/edgar/searchedgar/companysearch.html.

3. For a thoughtful early assessment on outsourcing, see James Brian Quinn and Frederick G. Hilmer (1995), "Strategic outsourcing," *McKinsey Quarterly* 1995 (1): 48–70.

4. "Is This the Factory of the Future?" Saul Hansell, *New York Times*, July 26, 1998, http://www.nytimes.com/1998/07/26/business/is-this -the-factory-of-the-future.html.

5. Figures are from the Bureau of Labor Statistics at http://www.bls.gov /data/#employment.

6. "By the Numbers: How Foxconn Churns Out Apple's iPhone 5s," Philip Elmer-Dewitt, *Fortune*, November 27, 2013, http://fortune.com /2013/11/27/by-the-numbers-how-foxconn-churns-out-apples -iphone-5s/.

7. "China's Troubling Robot Revolution," Martin Ford, *New York Times*, June 10, 2015, http://www.nytimes.com/2015/06/11/opinion/chinas -troubling-robot-revolution.html.

8. Dell's annual reports, with information on employment and strategy, are available at the SEC's EDGAR (for years prior to the company's going-private transaction): http://www.sec.gov/cgi-bin/browse-edgar?CIK =dell&Find=Search&owner=exclude&action=getcompany.

9. "101 Brand Names, 1 Manufacturer: The Mass Pet-Food Recall Reveals a Widespread Practice: Many Competing Products Come From the Same Factory," Ellen Byron, *Wall Street Journal*, May 9, 2007, http://www.wsj .com/articles/SB117867462888496739.

10. "Medicines Made in India Set Off Safety Worries," Gardiner Harris, *New York Times*, February 14, 2014, (http://www.nytimes.com/2014/02/15 /world/asia/medicines-made-in-india-set-off-safety-worries.html.

11. "US Identifies Tainted Heparin in 11 Countries," Gardiner Harris, *New York Times*, April 22, 2008, http://www.nytimes.com/2008/04/22 /health/policy/22fda.html?ref=todayspaper.

12. The Sara Lee story is recounted in Davis, *Managed by the Markets*. Sara Lee employment figures are available at the SEC's EDGAR: http://www.sec.gov/cgi-bin/browse-edgar?action=getcompany&CIK =0000023666&owner=exclude&count=40&hidefilings=0.

13. Yong Hyun Kim (2015), "Challenges for Global Supply Chain Sustainability: Evidence from the Conflict Minerals Reports" (unpublished manuscript, on file at the University of Michigan, Ross School of Business).

14. "How Goods Are Produced," Gerald F. Davis, *New York Times*, May 11, 2013; and "'Can Global Supply Chains Be Accountable?" Gerald F. Davis, *YaleGlobal Online*, May 16, 2013, http://yaleglobal.yale.edu /content/can-global-supply-chains-be-accountable.

15. "Inside Nike's Struggle to Balance Cost and Worker Safety in Bangladesh," Shelly Banjo, *Wall Street Journal*, April 21, 2014, http://www.wsj.com/news/articles /SB10001424052702303873604579493502231397942.

16. For more on the responsibility paradox, see Gerald F. Davis, Marina Whitman, and Mayer N. Zald (Winter 2008), "The responsibility paradox," *Stanford Social Innovation Review*, http://www.ssireview.org /articles/entry/the_responsibility_paradox/.

CHAPTER 7 THE PUBLIC CORPORATION BECOMES OBSOLETE

1. "U.S. Upstart Takes On TV Giants in Price War," Christopher Lawton, Yukari Iwatani Kane, and James Dean, *Wall Street Journal*, April 15, 2008, http://www.wsj.com/articles/SB120820684382013977.

2. "Vizio Dominates LCD TV Market in U.S.," Don Reisinger, CNET, February 24, 2011, http://www.cnet.com/news/vizio-dominates-lcd -tv-market-in-u-s/.

3. "A Tiny Camcorder Has a Big Payday," Ashlee Vance, *New York Times*, March 19, 2009, http://www.nytimes.com/2009/03/20/technology /companies/20flip.html; and "For Flip Video Camera, Four Years from Hot Start-up to Obsolete," Sam Grovart and Evelyn M. Rusli, *New York Times*, April 21, 2011, http://www.nytimes.com/2011/04/13 /technology/13flip.html.

4. "Sony's Bread and Butter? It's Not Electronics," Hiroko Tabuchi, *New York Times*, May 27, 2013, http://www.nytimes.com/2013/05/28 /business/global/sonys-bread-and-butter-its-not-electronics.html.

5. "The Internet's $10 Million Mix Tapes," Ethan Smith, *Wall Street Journal*, August 31, 2011, http://www.wsj.com/articles /SB10001424053111904009304576534711415540824#printMode.

6. For Netflix: http://www.sec.gov/Archives/edgar/data
    /1065280/000106528015000006/nflx201410k.htm.
    For Blockbuster: http://www.sec.gov/Archives/edgar/data
    /1085734/000119312505063510/d10k.htm.

7. John W. Meyer and Brian Rowan (1977), "Institutionalized organizations:
    Formal structure as myth and ceremony," *American Journal of Sociology*
    83:41–62.

8. ExxonMobil's proxy statement, including shareholder
    proposals, is available at http://www.sec.gov/Archives/edgar
    /data/34088/000119312515128602/d855824ddef14a.htm.

9. "Bay Watched: How San Francisco's New Entrepreneurial Culture Is
    Changing the Country," Nathan Heller, *The New Yorker*, October 14,
    2013, http://www.newyorker.com/magazine/2013/10/14/bay-watched.

CHAPTER 8 THE LAST GASP OF THE IPO MARKET

1. "Henry Ford Never Wanted His Company to Go Public," Jim Henry,
    Automotive News, June 16, 2003, http://www.autonews.com
    /article/20030616/SUB/306160730/henry-ford-never-wanted
    -his-company-to-go-public.

2. Professor Ritter's website at the Warrington College of Business is the
    authoritative resource for IPO data for the United States: http://site
    .warrington.ufl.edu/ritter/ipo-data/.

3. Data on IPOs is from Compustat, the Wharton Research Data Service,
    University of Pennsylvania, at https://wrds-web.wharton.upenn.edu
    /wrds/, and prospectuses accessed via the SEC's EDGAR database
    http://www.sec.gov/edgar/searchedgar/companysearch.html.

4. "The IPO Is Dying. Marc Andreessen Explains Why," Timothy B. Lee,
    Vox, June 26, 2014, http://www.vox.com/2014/6/26/5837638/the
    -ipo-is-dying-marc-andreessen-explains-why.

5. "Bay Watched," Heller, http://www.newyorker.com/magazine/2013
    /10/14/bay-watched.

6. Facebook's IPO prospectus is available from the SEC's EDGAR
    at http://www.sec.gov/Archives/edgar/data/1326801
    /000119312512034517/d287954ds1.htm.

7. Gerald F. Davis (2005), "New directions in corporate governance,"
    Annual Review of Sociology 31: 143–62.

8. Google's IPO prospectus is available at http://www.sec.gov/Archives
    /edgar/data/1288776/000119312504073639/ds1.htm.

9. Jay Ritter has compiled data on companies going public with dual-class voting shares at https://site.warrington.ufl.edu/ritter/files/2015/06/dual-class-ipo.pdf. Details for companies described here came from their prospectuses and proxy statements, accessed via the SEC's EDGAR at https://www.sec.gov/edgar/searchedgar/companysearch.html.

10. Facebook's prospectus, http://www.sec.gov/Archives/edgar/data/1326801/000119312512034517/d287954ds1.htm.

11. Data in this section came from the Compustat database maintained by the Wharton Research Data Services at https://wrds-web.wharton.upenn.edu/wrds/, and from corporate annual 10-K filings accessed via the SEC's EDGAR at https://www.sec.gov/edgar/searchedgar/companysearch.html.

12. These figures are based on my analyses of Compustat data and 10-K filings for IPO firms.

13. Shai Bernstein (August 2015), "Does going public affect innovation?" *Journal of Finance*, 70(4): 1365–1403 (Stanford Graduate School of Business, https://www.gsb.stanford.edu/faculty-research/publications/does-going-public-affect-innovation).

CHAPTER 9 THE DISAPPEARING SOCIAL SAFETY NET

1. The text of the original report by Sir William Beveridge, November 26, 1942, is available on the Socialist Health Association website at http://www.sochealth.co.uk/national-health-service/public-health-and-wellbeing/beveridge-report/.

2. Sanford M. Jacoby (1997), *Modern Manors: Welfare Capitalism Since the New Deal* (Princeton, New Jersey: Princeton University Press).

3. J. Adam Cobb (2012), *From the 'Treaty of Detroit' to the 401(k): The Development and Evolution of Privatized Retirement in the United States* (unpublished dissertation, University of Michigan); and Frank Levy and Peter Temin (2007), *Inequality and Institutions in 20th Century America* (Massachusetts Institute of Technology Department of Economics).

4. The classic statement of this argument is Oliver E. Williamson, Michael L. Wachter, and Jeffrey E. Harris (1975), "Understanding the employment relation: The analysis of idiosyncratic exchange," *Bell Journal of Economics* 6: 250–78.

5. "GM's Decision to Cut Pensions Accelerates Broad Corporate Shift: Benefits Curb Follows Path of Other Companies On Worker Guarantees," David Wessel, Ellen E. Schultz, and Laurie McGinley, *Wall Street Journal*, February 8, 2006, http://www.wsj.com/articles/SB113936666969167992.

6. "Retiree Benefits Take Another Hit: GM's Plan to End Medical Coverage For Many 65 and Over Signals a New Era; Pensions to Increase by $300 a Month," Vanessa Fuhrmans and Theo Francis, *Wall Street Journal*, July 16, 2008, http://www.wsj.com/articles/SB121617237912356653. See "Mom Gets Thrown Under the Bus by GM," July 18, 2008, for the text of the letter at http://www.dailykos.com/story/2008/07/19/553738/ -Mom-Gets-Thrown-Under-The-Bus-By-GM.

7. "Envisioning the End of Employer-Provided Health Plans," Neil Irwin, *New York Times*, May 1, 2014, http://www.nytimes.com/2014/05/01 /upshot/employer-sponsored-health-insurance-may-be-on-the-way-out .html?abt=0002&abg=0.

8. "Our Ridiculous Approach to Retirement," Theresa Ghilarducci, *New York Times*, July 21, 2012, http://www.nytimes.com/2012/07/22 /opinion/sunday/our-ridiculous-approach-to-retirement.html?ref =opinion.

9. See Davis, *Managed by the Markets*, (see chap. 1, n. 17), for details on changes in the largest employers.

10. Jonathan V. Hall and Alan B. Krueger (2015), "An Analysis of the Labor Market for Uber's Driver-Partners in the United States," January 22, 2015, http://dataspace.princeton.edu/jspui/bitstream/88435 /dsp010z708z67d/5/587.pdf.

11. Peer Hull Kristensen, "Globalization and the Nordic Model: Towards Enabling Welfare States and Experimental Systems of Economic Organization? Findings from the EU FP6 Project: Translearn," Interdisciplinary Committee on Organizational Studies, University of Michigan, October 2, 2009. His lecture is available for download at http://icos.umich.edu/lecture-2009-10-02.

CHAPTER 10 RISING INEQUALITY

1. "U.S. Income Inequality, on Rise for Decades, Is Now Highest since 1928," Drew DeSilver, Pew Research Center, December 5, 2013, http: //www.pewresearch.org/fact-tank/2013/12/05/u-s-income-inequality -on-rise-for-decades-is-now-highest-since-1928/.

2. "A Guide to Statistics on Historical Trends in Income Inequality," Chad Stone, Danilo Trisi, Arloc Sherman, and Brandon Debot, Center for Budget and Policy Priorities, February 20, 2015, http://www.cbpp.org /research/poverty-and-inequality/a-guide-to-statistics-on-historical -trends-in-income-inequality.

3. "Top CEOs Make 300 Times More Than Typical Workers," Lawrence Mishel and Alyssa Davis, Economic Policy Institute, June 21, 2015, http://www.epi.org/publication/top-ceos-make-300-times-more-than -workers-pay-growth-surpasses-market-gains-and-the-rest-of-the-0-1 -percent/.

4. "The Top 25 Hedge Fund Managers Earn More Than All Kindergarten Teachers in U.S. Combined," Philip Bump, *Washington Post*, May 12, 2015, http://www.washingtonpost.com/blogs/the-fix/wp/2015/05/12 /the-top-25-hedge-fund-managers-earn-more-than-all-kindergarten -teachers-combined/.

5. "Just How Wealthy Is the Wal-Mart Walton Family?" Tom Kertscher, Politifact, December 8, 2013, http://www.politifact.com/wisconsin /statements/2013/dec/08/one-wisconsin-now/just-how-wealthy -wal-mart-walton-family/.

6. See my talk on institutions and inequality at the Interdisciplinary Committee on Organizational Studies, University of Michigan, October 3, 2014, at http://icos.umich.edu/lecture-2014-10-03.

7. Thomas Piketty (2013), *Capital in the 21st Century* (Cambridge, MA: Belknap Press).

8. See the PayScale Human Capital website at http://www.payscale.com /data-packages/ceo-income/full-list

9. Herbert A. Simon (1957), "The compensation of executives," *Sociometry* 20: 32–5.

10. Gerald F. Davis and J. Adam Cobb (2010), "Corporations and economic inequality around the world: The paradox of hierarchy," *Research in Organizational Behavior* 30: 35–53.

11. Schumacher (1973), *Small Is Beautiful* (London: Blond and Briggs), 203.

CHAPTER 11 DECLINING UPWARD MOBILITY

1. "A Steep Slide in Law School Enrollments Accelerates," Elizabeth Olson and David Segal, *New York Times*, December 17, 2014, http://dealbook .nytimes.com/2014/12/17/law-school-enrollment-falls-to-lowest-level -since-1987/; and "Law School Is a Buyer's Market, with Top Students in Demand," Elizabeth Olson, *New York Times*, December 1, 2014, http: //dealbook.nytimes.com/2014/12/01/law-school-becomes-buyers -market-as-competition-for-best-students-increases/.

2. Drucker, "The new society I," 27 (see chap. 2, n. 13).

3. Markus Jantti, Knut Roed, Robyn Naylor, Anders Bjorklund, Bernt Bratsberg, et al. (2006), "American Exceptionalism in a New Light: A Comparison of Intergenerational Earnings Mobility in the Nordic Countries, the United Kingdom and the United States," (Bonn, Germany, Institute for the Study of Labor Discussion), Series Paper No. 1938, http://ftp.iza.org/dp1938.pdf.

4. A. D. Bernhardt, M. Morris, M. S. Handcock, and M. A. Scott (1999), *Job Instability and Wages for Young Adult Men*, Pennsylvania State University Working Paper No. 99-01; and "Promotion Track Fades for Those Starting at Bottom: Decline of In-House Training, Rise of Outsourcing Leave More Stuck in Menial Jobs," Joel Millman, *Wall Street Journal*, June 6, 2005, http://www.wsj.com/articles/SB111802315797151471.

5. For a brief summary, see "Upward Mobility Has Not Declined, Study Says," David Leonhardt, *New York Times*, January 23, 2014, http://www.nytimes.com/2014/01/23/business/upward-mobility-has-not-declined-study-says.html.

6. Paul Beaudry, David A. Green, and Benjamin M. Sand (2014), "The declining fortunes of the young since 2000," *American Economic Review* 104: 381–86.

7. "Jack Welch Class Day Interview—Jack Welch to HBS Grads: 'Don't Be a Jerk,'" Martha Lagace, Harvard Business School, Working Knowledge: The Thinking That Leads, June 11, 2011, http://hbswk.hbs.edu/archive/2310.html.

8. "Internships Abroad: Unpaid, with a $10,000 Price Tag," Steven Greenhouse, *New York Times*, February 5, 2015, http://www.nytimes.com/2015/02/08/education/edlife/the-10000-unpaid-global-internship.html.

9. "The Youngest Technorati," Matt Richtel, *New York Times*, March 8, 2014, http://www.nytimes.com/2014/03/09/technology/the-youngest-technorati.html.

10. "Pink Slips at Disney. But First, Training Foreign Replacements," Julia Preston, *New York Times*, June 3, 2015, http://www.nytimes.com/2015/06/04/us/last-task-after-layoff-at-disney-train-foreign-replacements.html?_r=0.

11. "Disney Layoffs and Immigrant Replacements Draw Deluge of Comments," Lela Moore, *New York Times*, June 5, 2015, http://www.nytimes.com/times-insider/2015/06/05/disney-layoffs-and-immigrant-replacements-draw-deluge-of-comments/.

12. "Young Workers Like Facebook, Apple, and Google," Rachel Emma Silverman, *Wall Street Journal*, November 13, 2011, http://www.wsj.com/articles/SB10001424052970203537304577032224274830372.

13. "Facebook Only Hired Seven Black People in Latest Diversity Count," Rupert Neate, *The Guardian*, June 25, 2015, http://www.theguardian .com/technology/2015/jun/25/facebook-diversity-report-black-white -women-employees.

14. See Apple's employment figures from its 2014 Securities and Exchange Commission 10-K at http://www.sec.gov/Archives/edgar/data/ 320193/000119312514383437/d783162d10k.htm; and "Apple's Retail Army, Long on Loyalty but Short on Pay," David Segal, *New York Times*, June 23, 2012, http://www.nytimes.com/2012/06/24/business/apple -store-workers-loyal-but-short-on-pay.html.

15. "The Youngest Technorati," Richtel, http://www.nytimes.com/2014 /03/09/technology/the-youngest-technorati.html.

16. "Why Do App Developers Still Live with Their Moms?" Gerald F. Davis, *Harvard Business Review*, March 26, 2014, https://hbr.org/2014/03/why -do-app-developers-still-live-with-their-moms.

CHAPTER 12 SILVER LININGS?

1. Yochai Benkler (2013), "Practical anarchism: Peer mutualism, market power, and the fallible state," *Politics & Society* 41: 213–51.

2. "There's an Uber for Everything Now," Geoffrey A. Fowler, *Wall Street Journal*, May 5, 2015, http://www.wsj.com/articles/theres-an-uber-for -everything-now-1430845789.

3. "Debating the Sharing Economy," Juliet Schor, Great Transition Initiative, October 2014, http://greattransition.org/publication/debating-the -sharing-economy.

4. "Buying Furniture on iTunes: Creative Destruction in a World of 'Locavore' Production," Network for Business Sustainability, November 7, 2012, http://nbs.net/buying-furniture-on-itunes-creative-destruction -in-a-world-of-locavore-production/.

5. Filson and Rohrbacher, AtFab, http://filson-rohrbacher.com/portfolio /atfab/.

6. "Here's the Firefox Smartphone—and Why It Exists," Nate Lanxon, Wired.co.uk, February 26, 2014, http://www.wired.co.uk/news /archive/2014-02-26/firefox-os-25.

7. "As More Tech Startups Stay Private, So Does the Money," Farhad Manjoo, *New York Times*, July 1, 2015, http://www.nytimes.com /2015/07/02/technology/personaltech/as-more-tech-start-ups-stay -private-so-does-the-money.html.

CHAPTER 13 POSSIBLE POSTCORPORATE FUTURES

1. Jeremy Rifkin (2011), *The Third Industrial Revolution: How Lateral Power Is Transforming Energy, Economy, and the World* (New York: Palgrave MacMillan).

2. Drucker, "The new society I," 21 (see chap. 2, n. 13).

3. Dr. Chuck Severance at the University of Michigan offers an excellent free online course in Python coding at https://online.dr-chuck.com/.

4. You can learn more about distributed manufacturing, and get involved yourself, at 100kGarages: http://www.100kgarages.com/.

5. Ronald H. Coase (1937), "The nature of the firm," *Economica* 4: 386–405.

6. "Modern Doctors' House Calls: Skype Chat and Fast Diagnosis," Abby Goodhough, *New York Times*, July 11, 2015, http://www.nytimes .com/2015/07/12/health/modern-doctors-house-calls-skype-chat-and -fast-diagnosis.html.

7. Gerald F. Davis (2010), "Job design meets organizational sociology," *Journal of Organizational Behavior* 31: 302–8.

8. "Computer Tablets Take Over Part of a Restaurant Server's Job," Stacy Vanek Smith, Planet Money, May 29, 2015, http://www.npr .org/2015/05/29/410470091/computer-tablets-take-over-part-of -restaurant-servers-job.

9. "Working Anything But 9 to 5: Scheduling Technology Leaves Low-Income Parents With Hours of Chaos," Jodi Kantor, *New York Times*, August 13, 2014, http://www.nytimes.com/interactive/2014/08/13 /us/starbucks-workers-scheduling-hours.html.

10. "Bosses Reclassify Workers to Cut Costs: Scrutiny into Relationships with Contractors Leads to New Strategies," Lauren Weber, *Wall Street Journal*, June 30, 2015, http://www.wsj.com/articles/bosses-reclassify -workers-to-cut-costs-1435688331.

11. "The People Inside Your Machine," NPR Planet Money, Episode 600, http://www.npr.org/templates/transcript/transcript.php?storyId =382657657.

12. Daniel Bell (1987), "The world and the United States in 2013," *Deadalus* 116(3): 1–31.

13. Benjamin R. Barber (2013), *If Mayors Ruled the World: Dysfunctional Nations, Rising Cities* (New Haven: Yale University Press).

14. Bill McKibben (2011), *Eaarth: Making a Life on a Tough New Planet* (New York: St. Martin's).

15. Jessica Gordon Nembhard (2014), *Collective Courage: A History of African American Cooperative Economic Thought and Practice* (University Park, PA: Pennsylvania State University Press).

16. See Gar Alperovitz (2013), *What Then Must We Do? Straight Talk about the Next American Revolution* (Chelsea Green Press).

CHAPTER 14 NAVIGATING A POSTCORPORATE ECONOMY

1. "A Steep Slide in Law School Enrollments Accelerates," Elizabeth Olson and David Segal, *New York Times*, December 17, 2014, http://dealbook .nytimes.com/2014/12/17/law-school-enrollment-falls-to-lowest-level -since-1987/.

2. "Is Success Even Possible in This 'Powerball' Economy?" Gerald F. Davis, Yahoo! Finance, December 17, 2012, http://finance.yahoo.com/blogs/the -exchange/success-even-possible-powerball-economy-233115628.html.

3. "Offshoring: The Next Industrial Revolution?" Alan S. Blinder, *Foreign Affairs*, March/April 2006, https://www.foreignaffairs.com /articles/2006-03-01/offshoring-next-industrial-revolution.

4. "Workers Stuck in Disability Stunt Economic Recovery," Leslie Scism and Jon Hilsenrath, *Wall Street Journal*, April 7, 2013, http://www.wsj .com/articles/SB1000142412788732351180457829815137453157; and "Trends with benefits," *This American Life*, Episode 490, March 22, 2013, http://www.thisamericanlife.org/radio-archives/episode/490/transcript.

5. "The Task Rabbit Economy," Robert Kuttner, *The American Prospect*, October 10, 2013, http://prospect.org/article/task-rabbit-economy.

6. Obama proposed this idea in his February 12, 2013, State of the Union address at https://www.whitehouse.gov/the-press-office/2013/02/12 /remarks-president-state-union-address; and see "Push to Gauge Bang for Buck from College Gains Steam," Ruth Simon and Michael Corkery, *Wall Street Journal*, February 11, 2013, http://www.wsj.com/articles /SB10001424127887324880504578298162378392502.

7. "Rick Scott wants to shift university funding away from some degrees," Zac Anderson, *Herald-Tribune*, October 10, 2011, http://politics .heraldtribune.com/2011/10/10/rick-scott-wants-to-shift-university -funding-away-from-some-majors/.

8. "Want a Steady Income? There's an App for That," Anand Giridharadas, *New York Times Magazine*, April 29, 2015, http://www.nytimes.com /2015/05/03/magazine/want-a-steady-income-theres-an-app-for-that .html.

9. "Replacing middle management with APIs," Peter Reinhardt, February 2015, http://rein.pk/replacing-middle-management-with-apis/.

INDEX

ABOUT THE AUTHOR

J**ERRY DAVIS HAS** spent the past 25 years trying to make sense of corporations: how they shape our lives, and how we shape them through laws, social movements, and internal activism. His formative influences include a youthful tour of the Ford Rouge Plant and stints as a sewer digger and a drill operator, all of which persuaded him that the life of the mind was a lot more appealing than actual work. After a series of dead-end jobs in the real world, he studied philosophy and psychology at the University of Michigan, business and sociology at Stanford, and taught at Northwestern and Columbia before returning home to the University of Michigan, where he is the Wilbur K. Pierpont Collegiate Professor of Management at the Ross School of Business, and Professor of Sociology. (It turns out that "tenured professor" is also a dead-end job, but never mind.)

Jerry is on the far end of the fox-hedgehog spectrum. He has published articles in architecture, economics, finance, law, management, politics, psychology, sociology, and strategy. He has served on dissertation committees in accounting, anthropology, architecture, education, English literature, finance, industrial engineering, information technology, kinesiology, management, marketing, natural resources, political science, psychology, public health, social work, sociology, and strategy.

It is possible that one day scientists will discover a treatment for this kind of thing; meanwhile, Jerry aims to promote and participate in conversations across disciplinary and other boundaries, particularly about how social scientists and activists can help midwife a more humane postcorporate future.

Jerry's previous books include *Social Movements and Organization Theory* (with Doug McAdam, W. Richard Scott, and Mayer N. Zald), a coedited collection on social movements; *Organizations and Organizing* (with W. Richard Scott), a text on organizations; *Managed by the Markets*, a book on how expansive financial markets maimed America, which won the Academy of Management's 2010 Terry Award for best book on management; and *Changing Your Company from the Inside Out* (with Christopher J. White), a guide for social intrapreneurs. Jerry is also the director of the Interdisciplinary Committee on Organization Studies (ICOS) and chief editor of *Administrative Science Quarterly*.

The Davis-Brown family divides its time between Ann Arbor and Detroit, and encourages you to visit Detroit for its great art, great architecture, great food, and great people.

You can reach Jerry at gfdavis@umich.edu.

Berrett–Koehler
Publishers

Berrett-Koehler is an independent publisher dedicated to an ambitious mission: *connecting people and ideas to create a world that works for all*.

We believe that to truly create a better world, action is needed at all levels—individual, organizational, and societal. At the individual level, our publications help people align their lives with their values and with their aspirations for a better world. At the organizational level, our publications promote progressive leadership and management practices, socially responsible approaches to business, and humane and effective organizations. At the societal level, our publications advance social and economic justice, shared prosperity, sustainability, and new solutions to national and global issues.

A major theme of our publications is "Opening Up New Space." Berrett-Koehler titles challenge conventional thinking, introduce new ideas, and foster positive change. Their common quest is changing the underlying beliefs, mindsets, institutions, and structures that keep generating the same cycles of problems, no matter who our leaders are or what improvement programs we adopt.

We strive to practice what we preach—to operate our publishing company in line with the ideas in our books. At the core of our approach is stewardship, which we define as a deep sense of responsibility to administer the company for the benefit of all of our "stakeholder" groups: authors, customers, employees, investors, service providers, and the communities and environment around us.

We are grateful to the thousands of readers, authors, and other friends of the company who consider themselves to be part of the "BK Community." We hope that you, too, will join us in our mission.

A BK Currents Book

This book is part of our BK Currents series. BK Currents books advance social and economic justice by exploring the critical intersections between business and society. Offering a unique combination of thoughtful analysis and progressive alternatives, BK Currents books promote positive change at the national and global levels. To find out more, visit **www.bkconnection.com**.

Berrett–Koehler
Publishers

Connecting people and ideas
to create a world that works for all

Dear Reader,

Thank you for picking up this book and joining our worldwide community of Berrett-Koehler readers. We share ideas that bring positive change into people's lives, organizations, and society.

To welcome you, we'd like to offer you a free e-book. You can pick from among twelve of our bestselling books by entering the promotional code **BKP92E** here: http://www.bkconnection.com/welcome.

When you claim your free e-book, we'll also send you a copy of our e-news-letter, the *BK Communiqué*. Although you're free to unsubscribe, there are many benefits to sticking around. In every issue of our newsletter you'll find

- A free e-book
- Tips from famous authors
- Discounts on spotlight titles
- Hilarious insider publishing news
- A chance to win a prize for answering a riddle

Best of all, our readers tell us, "Your newsletter is the only one I actually read." So claim your gift today, and please stay in touch!

Sincerely,

Charlotte Ashlock
Steward of the BK Website

Questions? Comments? Contact me at bkcommunity@bkpub.com.

Certified
B Corporation
bcorporation.net